Abundantly You

A Toolkit for Authentic Self-Care

Kelly Ayana Nembhard

Foreword by R. Kelly Crace, PhD

Dedication

To my grandfather
Victor Oliver Nembhard, Sr.
and
my great-grandmother
Anita "Miss Annie" Roberts

Our time was short, but your impact has been lifelong.

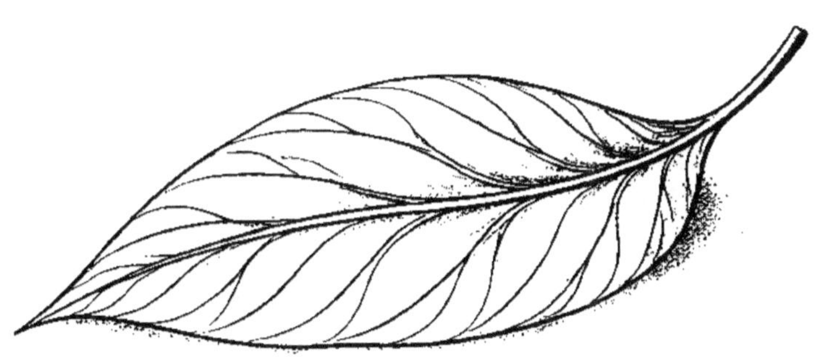

Table of Contents

Foreword

Kelly Nembhard's insightful guide to authentic self-care in *Abundantly You* could not be coming at a more crucial time. Our ecology of relentless pace, pressure, noise, and uncertainty has resulted in a stress glorification culture that leaves many overwhelmed and strained. Chasing calm has replaced chasing meaning. This desperate chasing of calm can often result in unhealthy, unmanaged self-soothing rather than authentic self-care. Kelly's creative and applicable approach provides a pathway back to authentic purpose, meaning, and wellbeing.

I have known Kelly for many years and have admired her courageous path as a scientist, wellness coach, and healer. Through each life chapter, she has done an exemplary job of integrating her experiences into a deeper level of awareness, purpose, and compassion. Faced with many rigid expectations and a harsh evaluative ecology, Kelly always fought for a more flexible, constantly evolving path that was values-centered instead of fear-centered. That approach is clearly reflected in this wonderful book. Kelly presents an approach that gives full agency and honor to the reader. Rather than being rigidly prescriptive, she provides space for the reader to focus on what speaks most to them, including the contextual sensitivity to the reader's motive – being a current critical situation, feeling overwhelmed in the moment, or a time of thoughtful reflection and repose. I am particularly drawn to the framework of distinguishing the Authentic Self and the Created Self, and found it to be a helpful current throughout the book. It would be easy to over-idealize one and devalue the other, but she does a wonderful job of explaining how both are important in our lives but require deeper attention, intention, and reflection to keep them in harmony.

I appreciate how Kelly brings her scientist-practitioner identity into this work. She presents information that is evidence-informed but in a manner that is practical and immediately applicable. So many personal growth and self-help books of today can eloquently speak to the factors that are causing us strain but fall short in how to address them or only provide surface-level solutions. In an age when wellness has been commodified and consumers struggle to know what to trust, Kelly provides an approach that honors the work of wellness and doesn't shy away from the ongoing intention and contemplation that is a part of that work. But she does it in a loving, compassionate manner that advocates for grace and self-compassion.

I value how Kelly brings full honor to the phenomenological perspective of the reader and is sensitive to socio-cultural influences that inform the work of authentic self-care. Her strategies are relevant to the full span of the neurodiversity continuum. She wasn't speaking to a particular type of brain but provided strategies that would be helpful no matter what gifts and challenges our brain brings to our life. While *Abundantly You* feels so suited for our times, I believe that if I pick her book up again and again over time (which I plan to do), it will feel just as relevant and applicable. Thank you, Kelly, for this gift.

Scope & Safety

Before we begin, I want to take a moment to talk about care, boundaries, and safety.

This book, *Abundantly You: A Toolkit for Authentic Self-Care*, is intended to support your growth through reflective practices, mindset work, emotional awareness, and holistic self-care tools. My intention is to offer guidance that helps you reconnect to yourself with more truth, gentleness, and empowerment.

That said, it is important for us to be clear about what this book is and what it is not.

THIS BOOK IS NOT MEDICAL CARE

The information in this book is provided for educational and self-help purposes only. It is not intended to diagnose, treat, cure, or prevent any disease or medical condition, and it should not be used as a substitute for professional medical advice, diagnosis, or treatment.

If you are experiencing symptoms that are severe, persistent, or concerning—physically or emotionally—please contact a qualified healthcare provider.

THIS BOOK IS NOT MENTAL HEALTH TREATMENT

Many of the practices in this toolkit may support emotional wellbeing, stress reduction, and self-awareness. However, this book does not replace therapy, psychiatric care, or professional mental health support.

If you are experiencing severe anxiety, depression, panic attacks, trauma symptoms, thoughts of self-harm, or any mental health crisis, please seek support immediately from a licensed mental health professional or local emergency services.

If you are in the United States and need immediate support, you can call or text 988 (Suicide & Crisis Lifeline).

USE YOUR INNER WISDOM

Throughout this book you will be invited to experiment with different tools—such as journaling, meditation, breathwork, visualization, energy-based practices, rest, and gentle lifestyle shifts.

Please remember:

- Your body is wise.
- Your nervous system deserves compassion.
- You are allowed to move slowly.

You do not need to force yourself through any practice that doesn't feel safe or supportive.

If anything in this book feels overwhelming, activating, or destabilizing, pause and return to what helps you feel grounded. That may include resting, drinking water, stepping outside for fresh air, talking to a trusted friend, or seeking professional support.

A NOTE ABOUT HOLISTIC PRACTICES

This book includes holistic self-care approaches that may involve spiritual, energetic, or mind-body perspectives. These practices are not intended to replace medical care. They are offered as supportive tools that many people find helpful for stress reduction, self-connection, and overall wellbeing.

If you are pregnant, nursing, taking medication, managing a chronic condition, or under medical supervision, always consult a qualified healthcare provider before making major changes to your wellness routine.

Self-care is not about perfection.

It's about presence.

It's about learning how to come home to yourself—one small choice at a time.

Take what resonates.

Leave what doesn't.

And always choose what supports your safety and wellbeing.

If You're Struggling Right Now

Y

ou don't have to read this entire book to benefit from it. If you're in crisis, overwhelmed, or barely holding on, start here.

- **If you're emotionally overwhelmed**: Turn to "Self-Care Tip: Ground & Center" (page 47). This article offers immediate techniques to calm your nervous system and bring you back to the present moment.
- **If you're physically exhausted or burnt out**: Turn to "Take a Break" (page 17). This article gives you permission to rest—and explains why honoring that need is wisdom, not weakness.
- **If you've pushed past your limits**: Turn to "Know Your Limits Before You Cross Them" (page 16). This article helps you understand your capacity and recognize the signs that you've exceeded it.
- **If you need reassurance that you'll be okay**: Turn to "All is Well" (page 212). This article offers a simple breathing technique and a reminder that you've survived every difficult day so far.
- **If you're experiencing a mental health crisis**: Turn to "Self-Care Tip: When to Seek Professional Help" (page 106). This article helps you recognize when self-care isn't enough and guides you toward professional support.

It's okay to not be okay. You found this book at the right time. Relief is possible—not by doing everything at once, but by taking one small step. Start with whichever article speaks to what you're feeling right now. The rest will be here when you're ready.

Introduction

The mind chatter was deafening that afternoon as I walked from the hospital cafeteria back to the lab. My project wasn't working. I hated being there. I imagined what everyone thought about my lack of progress. I wondered what they'd say if I quit. The noise in my head was so loud I felt like I was going crazy.

Then I remembered what my therapist had said. My symptoms were typical of prison inmates. Tension headaches. Muscle spasms. Irritable bowel syndrome. Rashes and random vomiting. Hair loss. My body was screaming that something was wrong. But I'd kept pushing through. For eight and a half years, I'd been trying to finish a Ph.D. in Cell and Developmental Biology. I was researching the genetics of birth defects affecting the heart. Every time my project hit a dead end, I told myself I'd come too far to quit. Every time I considered leaving with a master's degree, someone told me my life would amount to nothing. Or that I'd be wasting everyone's time.

So I stayed. Not because I wanted to become a professor or run my own lab. I'd figured out years ago that I had no interest in either. I didn't even want to see another lab coat or pipette. I just knew I wanted to use biology to help people. And I believed I needed that Ph.D. to do it.

Walking back to the lab that day, I heard a question break through the noise. It was my voice, but it felt like someone else was speaking to me: *Why would anyone who cares about you want you to sacrifice your health to get a degree that no longer mattered to you?*

The impact felt physical. Like a winning goal scored in the final second of a match. Like someone shouting "FINALLY, SHE ASKED THE RIGHT QUESTION!" The mind chatter quieted. The chaos parted like the Red Sea. One clear realization came through: no one who genuinely cares about me would want this sacrifice.

Then came the next question, still in my voice but directed at me: *What's the worst that could happen if you quit?*

My mind went completely blank. I couldn't think of anything worse than the hell I was already enduring.

That's when I understood. I'd been living my entire life trying to meet everyone else's expectations. I thought meeting those expectations would make me happy. But I'd been in a constant state of seeking happiness and never arriving. I was staying in graduate school for other people, not for myself.

The day I officially left with my master's degree, I felt like I was floating on cloud nine. Then, throughout the day, I went to my graduate school colleagues one by one to tell them. I watched their faces shift to irritation the moment I told them. They turned their backs on me. Literally. Some of them were people I used to hug goodbye every time we parted. They turned away before I could even offer that hug. I was simply dismissed.

I expected to feel devastated. I'd feared this rejection for years. But instead, I felt... nothing. Just a strange indifference, like I was checking something off my to-do list. I noticed my own reaction and wondered why I felt so little.

That evening, a "friend" cursed at me in a room full of people. He told me to mind my "fucking business" over a simple question I'd asked. In that moment, everything clicked. This person had been verbally and mentally abusive to me for years. I decided right then to cut him out of my life.

The colleagues who turned their backs and this "friend" who'd always treated me poorly—suddenly I could see clearly. None of them were ever really my friends. That's why their rejection felt like nothing. Freeing myself from the dungeon of graduate school had lifted a fog I didn't know was there. I'd been so caught up in unhappiness and desperation that I couldn't see what was right in front of me. I'd spent years worrying about people who never actually contributed to my life.

Even now, there are loved ones who believe I should have never quit the program. I recognize their belief isn't about me. They're likely trying to find happiness through me. And that's not my responsibility.

Six weeks later, I had a job in clinical research. I was using biology to help people without needing that Ph.D. I had no regrets about leaving. I walked away with valuable skills, lifelong friends, and the first step toward living as my Authentic Self.

Your path may look different from mine. You might not need to quit anything. But if you're exhausting yourself trying to meet others' expectations, if your body is sending signals you keep ignoring, if you're chasing a version of success that doesn't actually matter to you—this book is for you.

And if you're afraid that living authentically will cost you your community, I want you to know something: when people turn their backs on you for being yourself, you might discover the rejection doesn't hurt the way you feared it would. Because your Authentic Self already knows who your real people are. The fear of losing them is often worse than actually losing them. And what you gain—your freedom, your health, your peace—is worth far more than their approval ever was.

The journey from that pivotal question to genuine self-care taught me something crucial: your well-being isn't selfish. It's the foundation for everything else. This book shares what I learned about caring for your Authentic Self—the version of you that exists beneath all those external expectations. Those questions I heard that day? They came from my Authentic Self speaking to me. This book will help you hear yours too.

How to Use This Book

You don't have to read this book cover to cover. It's designed so you can:

- Start with any article that speaks to where you are right now
- Use "If You're Struggling Right Now" as a quick reference when you're in crisis
- Read one section at a time, taking breaks to practice what resonates
- Return to articles as your needs change over time

Each article in this book ends with an Intention of the Day—not just something to read, but something to practice. You'll also find Self-Care Tips throughout the book. At the end of the book, you'll find Your Self-Care Toolkit, which helps you apply what you've learned by taking inventory of your practices and planning how to use them. Return to these pages whenever you need them—your needs will shift, and the articles that matter most to you will shift too.

Throughout the book, you'll encounter two main concepts: your **Authentic Self** and your **Created Self**. Don't worry if these terms are unfamiliar—the next section explains them fully. For now, just know that this book is about reconnecting with who you actually are beneath all the expectations you've absorbed from others.

Key Terms

Before you begin, here are the core concepts you'll see throughout this book:

- **Authentic Self:** The version of you that exists independent of others' expectations. It observes neutrally and decides what's true for you, forming its own beliefs while accepting consequences without fear.

- **Created Self:** The version of you shaped by others' expectations and by your response to fear or trauma. It's not fake—you genuinely believe these adopted values are yours. The Created Self helps you navigate social situations and maintain relationships. You need it.

- **Authentic Self-Care:** Attention to improving and maintaining your whole health in ways that align with your Authentic Self. It's multidimensional (career, physical, mental, emotional, environmental, social, spiritual) and honors your beliefs and values rather than following someone else's prescription.

- **The Seven Dimensions of Health:** Career, Physical, Mental, Emotional, Environmental, Social, and Spiritual health. These dimensions don't operate independently—when one suffers, the others feel the impact.

These concepts will be explored in depth throughout the book. For now, this gives you the foundation you need to understand what comes next.

What is the Authentic Self?

Have you ever caught yourself saying what you thought someone wanted to hear instead of what you actually believed? Have you changed your opinion mid-conversation because you sensed disapproval? When you make choices—what to wear, what to study, how to spend your time—are you choosing based on what genuinely feels right to you or what you think you should want?

Most of us don't realize we're living from two different versions of ourselves. Understanding the difference between them changes everything.

Since childhood, people have told you how to be. Family told you how to feel. Teachers told you what to value. Culture prescribed everything from your diet to your hairstyle to your role in society. When you didn't comply, you faced shame, judgment, or even attack. To avoid that pain, you learned to adopt these expectations as your own. You became what others wanted rather than discovering who you actually are.

This is the Created Self in action—the version you've been living from without realizing there was another option. Now that you understand this split exists, the next question is: how do you recognize which version is operating? How can you tell when it's your Created Self responding versus your Authentic Self? When someone says red is bad, your Created Self might immediately agree to avoid conflict. Your Authentic Self pauses and asks: What is red? What qualities does it have? How does it affect the world? How does it make me feel?

Your Authentic Self forms its own beliefs and expresses them while accepting the consequences without fear. It might decide it loves red and choose to bring red into your life—even knowing others dislike it.

Remember those questions I heard walking back to the lab? *Why would anyone who cares about you want you to sacrifice your health?* That was my Authentic Self speaking. It cut through years of conditioning to reveal what I actually knew to be true.

Here's what's important: your Authentic Self and Created Self aren't at war. They coexist, and you need both. Imagine your friend hates red, and you love it. You can honor your Authentic Self by wearing red shoes to their birthday party. At the same time, your Created Self prompts you to give them a gift that's not red. You're being authentically you while thoughtfully navigating the relationship. This balance allows you to honor yourself while considering others.

Living authentically doesn't mean ignoring social norms or others' feelings. It doesn't mean being selfish or rude. It means making conscious choices about when and how to adapt, rather than automatically performing what you think others expect. It means knowing the difference between genuine care for others and people-pleasing out of fear.

Living primarily from your Created Self means constantly performing for approval—exhausting yourself trying to be what others want. Your Authentic Self operates from inner clarity rather than external validation. That's where genuine fulfillment lives.

The more you express your Authentic Self, the more happiness and inner peace become possible. The Created Self helps you navigate the world, but your Authentic Self is where your true life happens. But how do you recognize when your Authentic Self is speaking? Sometimes it happens in quiet moments of clarity. Other times, it emerges when lived experience challenges what you've been taught to believe.

Recognizing Your Authentic Self

How do you know when your Authentic Self is speaking?

I grew up in Jamaica, where Christian culture tolerated gay men only if they stayed invisible. The moment they were open about who they were, tolerance shifted to rejection and hostility. Despite being a Christian, I never understood it. The negativity made no sense to me, but I had no way to test what I'd been taught until I visited Wesleyan University before enrolling.

That's where I met Bryon. He was openly gay—loud, sweet, fun, and welcoming. A few minutes after meeting him, I thought to myself, "Well, I didn't burst into flames. So I'm good!" When I started at Wesleyan a few months later, we became friends.

The following spring, I sprained my ankle badly. The campus center was too far to walk to for breakfast without making my injury worse. On a Friday evening, I asked four friends separately if they could bring me breakfast Saturday morning. I asked them each alone so no one knew I'd asked the others. All four said yes. But Bryon was the only one who actually showed up.

That breakfast delivery made me think about another chapter of my life—when everything turned upside down because of my grandfather's murder.

My grandfather was gentle and playful. I remember the day I accidentally hit his golf ball under the bed while "practicing" in his room. I couldn't reach it, so I left it there and hoped he wouldn't notice. He called me in later, holding the golf club. I was terrified. Every Jamaican child knows to fear adults with discipline on their minds. But instead of punishment, he handed me the club and calmly said, "Take the club and roll the ball from under the bed." After I retrieved it, he pulled me into a big bear hug and sent me on my way.

He was seventy-six years old when two young men robbed him, kidnapped him, beat him, shot him, and buried him in a shallow grave. I was ten.

Those two men who murdered my grandfather weren't gay. They weren't white, Muslim, rich, poor, or any of the identities I'd been taught to be wary of. They were simply two people who valued pride and money over human life and dignity.

When Bryon brought me breakfast that morning, these pieces came together in my mind. I decided then and there that I had no energy to feel negatively about someone's race, ethnicity, culture, gender, sexual orientation, religion, political beliefs, education, or social status. My only concern would be the condition of a person's soul and the hurt they inflict on other people's lives.

This was my earliest memory of letting my Authentic Self step forward. It rejected cultural prejudice and chose to judge people by their character. Your Authentic Self will do the same—cutting through what you've been taught to reveal what you actually know to be true.

What is Authentic Self-Care?

Now that you understand what your Authentic Self is and how to recognize when it speaks, the question becomes: how do you care for it?

Imagine you're working long hours on an important project. The deadline looms, so you stay late at the office night after night. You're not getting enough sleep, and when you finally get to bed, your mind races with everything left undone.

During my training as a health coach at Duke Integrative Medicine, I learned that this scenario reveals something crucial: your health isn't compartmentalized.

Notice what's happening in this situation. The stress from work affects your sleep. Poor sleep makes it harder to focus, which creates more work stress. You feel frustrated and overwhelmed. You barely have energy to tidy your home, so clutter accumulates. When you do spend time with friends or family, you're too exhausted to truly enjoy their company. You feel disconnected from what matters most to you, as if you're just surviving rather than living with purpose.

One problem has cascaded across your entire life. That's because your well-being depends on seven interconnected factors, and when one suffers, the others feel the impact.

Career health addresses your work-life balance, your ability to meet goals, and how well your work aligns with your values. In this scenario, an important project has consumed your life. See how career health affects everything else?

Physical health includes how your body moves, refuels, and repairs—your exercise, nutrition, sleep, and ability to care for yourself. When work stress disrupts your sleep, your physical health declines. Notice how physical and career health are already affecting each other?

Mental health involves how you process information and experiences. Your racing thoughts at night, your difficulty concentrating at work—that's your mental health struggling under the weight of stress. See how mental health connects to both physical and career health?

Emotional health refers to your ability to identify and express your feelings appropriately. The frustration and overwhelm you're experiencing? That's your emotional health responding to the strain on your physical, mental, and career health.

Environmental health means how your physical surroundings affect your quality of life—your home, workplace, and the spaces you inhabit. When you're too exhausted to maintain your home, clutter builds. That cluttered environment adds to your stress, which circles back to affect your mental and emotional health.

Social health is your ability to form and maintain meaningful relationships. When you're with loved ones but too drained to engage, your social health suffers. And without that connection, you lose an important source of support that could help you manage the work stress.

Spiritual health is your ability to maintain inner peace and clarity even amid life's challenges. It's when your heart feels calm, your purpose feels clear, and you can face difficulties without losing your center. When you feel disconnected from what matters most—when you're just surviving instead of living with meaning—your spiritual health is depleted.

Notice how one issue with work has affected all seven dimensions of your health. And see how these dimensions don't just decline independently—they drag each other down in a cascade effect.

Here's another example. Maybe you have chronic knee pain that makes it difficult to clean your home. Over time, clutter and dust accumulate. The dust triggers your allergies, so now you're constantly coughing and sneezing. Your physical health (knee pain) affected your environmental health (cluttered home), which circled back to worsen your physical health (allergies). Depending on how long this continues, your emotional health might suffer next (frustration or sadness about your home's condition). Then perhaps your social health (embarrassment about inviting people over).

This is the interconnected nature of whole health.

Some concerns cut across multiple dimensions. Financial stress is one of them. When money feels chaotic, it affects your mental health through worry, your emotional health through shame or fear, your social health through strain on relationships, and even your physical health through stress-related symptoms. That's why budgeting isn't just about numbers—it's self-care that touches nearly every part of your well-being.

Take a moment and think about your own life. When was the last time stress in one area affected another? What cascades have you experienced? Which dimension of your health tends to suffer first when you're overwhelmed?

Most self-care advice treats these dimensions as separate—exercise for physical health, meditation for mental health—as if they're independent tasks on a checklist. But your health doesn't work that way. Everything connects. And what's more: you're unique. What works for someone else might not work for you. Following trends or copying others' practices without asking if they serve you isn't authentic self-care.

Authentic self-care is attention to improving and maintaining your whole health in ways that align with your Authentic Self. It's self-care that's multidimensional and multifactorial, just like your health. It honors the beliefs and values of your Authentic Self rather than following someone else's prescription.

Going to a hair salon might be self-care for one person but a stressful obligation for another. Two people might both value physical exercise but pursue it differently—one through gym workouts, another through dancing. One person finds spiritual health through religious practice while another finds it through time in nature. There are over eight billion people on this planet, which means there are over eight billion versions of authentic self-care.

Some dimensions of health may be more foundational for you than others—and discovering which ones is part of authentic self-care. For one person, environmental health is foundational; they can't function well without an organized space. For another, social health matters most; they need regular connection with their tribe to feel whole. Your Authentic Self determines what's foundational for you.

Throughout this book, you'll discover how to care for each dimension in ways that honor who you truly are. You'll learn to recognize which dimensions need attention and how interconnections work in your specific life. You'll find tools for breaking cascade effects before they overwhelm you. Most importantly, you'll learn to distinguish between what you genuinely need and what you think you should want.

You'll also find Self-Care Tips throughout these pages—invitations to explore potential tools for your authentic self-care, not directives you must follow. You won't use every tip in this book, and that's not just okay—it's expected. If a tip doesn't feel right to you, that's valuable information about what doesn't serve your Authentic Self. Even rejecting a suggestion teaches you something important about who you are. The goal is to offer options you might not have considered or to illuminate benefits of practices you've heard about but never tried. And remember: what doesn't feel right now might speak to you in a different season of life. Your authentic self-care toolkit will be uniquely yours, and it will evolve as you do.

The following sections explore each dimension of your health, offering articles and practices you can adapt to your authentic self-care journey. Start wherever you are. Take what resonates. Leave what doesn't.

Section 1: Your Vehicle

Care for your physical and mental foundation

Know Your Limits Before You Cross Them

Every human being has limits. The question is: do you know yours? Think about your work capacity. Maybe you can efficiently handle four projects at the same time—you're focused, productive, and meeting deadlines with quality work. But when you take on a fifth project, you become forgetful and prone to mistakes. That difference between four and five? That's your limit talking. This knowledge gives you the power to set clear boundaries around your workload with your manager and colleagues.

I learned this lesson as a health coach. I discovered the maximum number of coaching calls I could do in a day is seven. More than seven, it became hard to focus on what the client was saying. It became harder to brainstorm ideas with them. I would also make more typing errors when writing my progress notes. My limit wasn't arbitrary—it was the point where my ability to truly serve my clients began to decline.

Your body and mind are constantly communicating your limits through signs like fatigue, irritability, difficulty concentrating, or physical tension. The key is paying attention to these signals before they become chronic problems, like high blood pressure. Otherwise, you'll end up adding "managing high blood pressure" to your already long to-do list. That puts more distance between you and your happiness.

Knowing your actual limits allows you to take care of and protect yourself. This is the foundation of living a long, happy, and healthy life. When you honor your limits, you're not being lazy or inadequate—you're being wise. You're choosing to sustain your well-being instead of depleting it.

Intention of the Day
I will know my limits well enough to avoid crossing them today.

Take a Break

Sometimes you push through exhaustion to meet a deadline or prove a point. Other times, you keep going because you're "in the zone." But what about when you're truly tired, sick, or overwhelmed?

Here's what often happens: despite knowing better, you push through anyway and end up burnt out—of no use to yourself or others. Why? Because taking a break can feel like admitting weakness, laziness, or failure.

Your body sends clear signals when it needs rest. Over the years, I discovered that when I felt fatigued for no apparent reason, it meant I needed to take the day off and just relax. Whenever I ignored that signal and pushed through, I was always sick the very next day with an infection. My body wasn't being dramatic—it was giving me advance warning.

Your Authentic Self knows the difference between fatigue that needs rest and fatigue that needs movement. It knows when pushing through serves you and when it depletes you. The key is learning to trust those signals instead of overriding them with what you think you should be able to handle.

Think about what your body might be telling you right now. Exhaustion isn't always about needing more sleep—sometimes it's your system saying it needs a break from stress, stimulation, or constant doing. When you honor that need, you're not being weak. You're being wise. You're preventing the breakdown that comes from running on empty.

Taking a break isn't about giving up. It's about giving yourself what you need so you can keep going in ways that actually sustain you. Your well-being isn't selfish—it's the foundation for everything else.

Intention of the Day
I will listen when my body signals rest, trusting this protects my long-term capacity.

The Mind-Body Connection

How does your body usually react to unwanted or negative experiences? A clenched jaw? A leg spasm? Tightness in your throat or a knot in your stomach? Does your focus shift when you're tired, sick, or in pain? Our mind and body communicate constantly, each affecting how the other functions. When one struggles, the other often follows. This mind-body connection helps you identify your stressors and reveals how well you're handling them. Being aware of this connection is the first step toward protecting your physical and emotional well-being during life's challenges.

Our bodies are excellent communicators. They signal when our mental health is compromised. The problem is what happens when we ignore those warnings. When I was struggling in graduate school, I experienced frequent bloating and abdominal pain. I accepted it as a normal response to the stress of the Ph.D. program, so I did nothing to address it. I ignored the fact that I was exceeding my stress limit. The consequence? Years of IBS and gastritis that persisted long after I left graduate school.

Your body is trying to tell you something. To understand what it's saying, try this: during an uncomfortable experience, take one minute to close your eyes and scan your body. Notice which parts feel tight, painful, or heavy. Once you identify an area of discomfort, take three deep, gentle breaths at your own pace. Imagine inhaling healing energy into that area and exhaling the tension.

The more you practice this technique, the easier it becomes for your body to relax. Your awareness of stress responses will sharpen. You may even begin noticing your body reacting to stressors you weren't consciously aware of before.

Intention of the Day
I will scan my body for tension and breathe healing into it.

Spoil Your Body

Your body is a trusted guide. It takes you on a tour of human life. And like any trusted companion who works tirelessly for you, your body deserves to be spoiled—not just maintained, but celebrated and delighted.

When you face daily struggles, your body works hard to keep you safe. It keeps going even when you lack sleep, eat poorly, feel stressed, or overuse your joints and muscles.

Since your body works so hard, think about how you treat it. Do you give it the care it needs? More importantly, do you care for your body because you have to or because you want to? That difference—between obligation and desire—is the difference between maintaining a relationship and truly honoring it. Are you ignoring its messages, such as fatigue, belly pains, or high blood sugar? Do you pay attention to the lessons, such as scars, that it teaches you?

Your connection with your body is the most important relationship you will ever have. It is also the longest. Friends will come and go. Careers will change. Your body stays with you at all times. It is there in sickness and in health until death do you part. Like any close relationship, this one needs care. Communicate and respect your physical limits. Trust that the messages your body sends are important. Be patient when you want your body to adapt to new circumstances. Be consistent with your self-care. If you treat your body well, it will repay you by giving you the best tour of life possible.

Your body knows what it truly needs. When you listen and respond with care, you honor the relationship that matters most.

Intention of the Day
I will spoil my body today so that it knows I value all it does for me.

Self-Care Tip: Hydrate

Your body is mostly water. Every cell, every organ, and every function depends on it. Water helps carry nutrients to where they are needed. It also helps remove waste, cushion your joints, and keep your temperature steady. When you are well hydrated, your body can work better and recover more easily. You may also find it easier to handle stress.

I learned this after a Reiki healing session. Seven people worked on me for about five minutes. The next morning, I woke up with strong congestion, a sore throat, and sinus pain. It came on suddenly, which felt strange.

When I looked into it, I learned that some people report feeling "off" after deep healing work. In my case, I realized I had not been drinking enough water. At that time, I was drinking about forty ounces of water a day. I drank two glasses within an hour. Soon after, I felt much better.

This experience showed me how much my body needs water to feel supported.

When you are dehydrated, your body has to work much harder. You may feel low energy or dizziness. You may notice constipation, dry skin, or brittle hair. Severe dehydration is serious and may require medical care. If your symptoms are strong, sudden, or do not go away, please reach out to a healthcare professional.

One simple way to check your hydration is to look at your urine color. If it is light, like lemonade, you are likely hydrated. If it is darker, more like amber, you may need more water.

Here are some ways to drink more throughout your day. Place a water bottle in each room as a reminder. Set phone alarms or use a tracking app. Keep a bottle in your car to sip at red lights. If plain water feels boring, add cucumber, mint, or berries for flavor. Unsweetened herbal teas can help you stay hydrated too. Eating fresh fruits and vegetables also helps, since they have high water content.

Your body would not be made mostly of water if it were not important. Staying hydrated supports everything your body does to keep you well. If you're not used to drinking water, start with one extra glass a day.

Stretch for a Happy Body

For eight years, chronic knee pain and surgery kept me from being able to squat. I worked around it by bending at the waist instead. I had stopped even trying to squat. The fear of pain kept me stuck, and I accepted this as my new normal.

Then I started stretching five minutes every day. Two months later, I was cooking and needed something from a lower cabinet. Without thinking, I squatted down, grabbed what I needed, and stood back up. I froze. I had just done something my body had not done in eight years. My body remembered what my mind had forgotten was possible. Two months undid eight years of fear and stagnation.

Stretching is essential for a healthy body. It helps with injury recovery and prevents new injuries. It improves flexibility, increases blood flow to your muscles, and relieves stress. After long periods of sitting or lying down, it resets your joints to proper alignment. Stretching your neck and shoulder muscles also eases tension headaches.

When did you last move beyond sitting, walking, and lying down? Modern life keeps us in a narrow range of motion, but our bodies are designed for much more. Without regular stretching, your body loses the ability to move freely and will eventually protest.

Make it a goal to stretch today. If you are ready to start, here are some ways to begin safely. Ask your doctor for suggestions. Join a beginner yoga or Pilates class. Search YouTube for videos on stretching for beginners. Visit a certified stretch practitioner for an assessment and personalized recommendations. You can also stretch in your car or at your desk. Try setting a reminder on your work calendar or smartphone to take a few minutes each day. Start small, stay consistent, and notice what becomes possible.

Intention of the Day
I will stretch today to honor my body's need for movement.

Self-Care Tip: Movement Beyond Stretching

In "Stretch for a Happy Body," you explored how stretching restores flexibility and releases tension. But your body is designed for more than sitting, walking, and stretching. It's built to climb, dance, lift, and play. When you limit your movement to the bare minimum, you miss opportunities for joy, connection, and strength that support your whole health.

Movement isn't just physical self-care. It affects your mental and emotional well-being too. Exercise releases endorphins that lift your mood. It burns off stress hormones that accumulate during difficult days. It improves sleep, sharpens focus, and builds confidence. The key is finding movement that feels like a gift to your body rather than a punishment.

For years, I hated going to the gym. But I loved movement. While I was in graduate school, I discovered forms of exercise that didn't feel like exercise at all. Salsa dancing gave me cardio while allowing me to socialize and express creativity—not just through dance, but through changing my wardrobe, hair, and makeup each week when I went out. Indoor climbing let me build strength and flexibility while experiencing a sense of achievement every time I made it further up the wall than before. Pilates helped me gain strength in everyday movements—getting up from a chair, lifting heavy grocery bags, reaching above my head to put something in a cabinet. None of these felt like chores. They felt like play.

Your Authentic Self knows what kind of movement suits you. Here are some options to explore:

Walking and Hiking

The simplest form of movement is also one of the most powerful. Walking connects you with nature, promotes grounding, and invites presence. You don't need special equipment or a gym membership. A twenty-minute walk around your neighborhood or a weekend hike in a local park counts. Let your pace match your energy rather than forcing intensity.

DANCING

Dancing combines cardio with creativity and self-expression. You can take a class—salsa, hip-hop, ballroom, Zumba—or simply turn on music in your living room and move however your body wants. Dancing with others adds social connection. Dancing alone offers freedom to express without judgment.

STRENGTH TRAINING AND WEIGHT LIFTING

Building muscle does more than change your appearance. It supports bone density, improves posture, and boosts metabolism. You can lift weights at a gym, use resistance bands at home, or work with your own body weight through exercises like squats and push-ups. Start where you are and progress gradually.

YOGA AND PILATES

Beyond their stretching benefits, yoga and Pilates build core strength, improve balance, and train flexibility alongside strength. These practices teach body awareness—noticing how you hold tension, where you lack stability, how breath supports movement. Classes are widely available in studios, gyms, and online.

FUNCTIONAL EXERCISE

Functional movements train your body for daily life—lifting, reaching, bending, carrying. These exercises maintain joint strength and flexibility as you age, reducing injury risk and keeping you capable of tasks that matter. Squats, lunges, and rotational movements all fall into this category. A physical therapist or personal trainer can help you identify which functional exercises serve your specific needs.

PLAYFUL MOVEMENT

Remember what it felt like to move as a child—climbing, jumping, chasing, tumbling? Playful movement brings that joy back. Play tag with your kids or grandkids. Throw a ball for your dog and race them to fetch it. Try indoor climbing and experience the achievement of reaching the top. Jump on a trampoline. Playful movement offers quality time with those you love while reminding your body what it's capable of.

FINDING WHAT FITS YOUR AUTHENTIC SELF

You don't have to love running just because others swear by it. You don't have to join a gym if gyms feel intimidating. Your movement practice should reflect who you are and what brings you alive.

Ask yourself: What did I enjoy as a child? What sounds fun rather than obligatory? What would I do if no one were watching or judging? The answers point toward movement that will sustain you long-term—not because you force yourself, but because you genuinely want to show up.

Your body has carried you through every moment of your life. Honor it by letting it move in ways that feel like celebration rather than punishment.

Your Relationship with Food

Food is nourishment. But for many of us, it's also complicated—tangled with emotions, memories, beliefs, and judgments that have little to do with hunger or health.

Your Created Self often drives unhealthy eating patterns. Maybe you learned that cleaning your plate earned approval. Maybe food became comfort when emotions felt too big to handle. Maybe you absorbed messages about "good" and "bad" foods that turned eating into a moral test you constantly fail. Maybe you eat quickly when stressed, barely tasting what's in front of you. These patterns aren't character flaws. They're adaptations—ways your Created Self learned to cope, please others, or protect you from pain.

I know this struggle personally. I have many food allergies and sensitivities. I'm also a picky eater when it comes to textures. Eating around others makes me self-conscious—I wonder what people think about my food choices. I feel frustrated and sad that I can't eat foods I used to enjoy before my body changed. I carry guilt about not being able to afford healthier options like organic produce. For a long time, meals felt like a minefield of judgment, loss, and limitation.

What helped me shift was bringing intention and presence to eating. Before each meal, I pause to bless my food with the intention that it will serve my body well. You might do this through prayer, gratitude, or simply a quiet moment of acknowledgment. This small ritual transforms eating from obligation into care. I also notice how fast I'm eating, especially when stressed—rushing through meals irritates my gastritis, so slowing down protects my health.

How Created Self Beliefs Affect Eating

As you will explore in "Understanding Overindulgence," reaching for food often has nothing to do with hunger. You might eat to numb difficult emotions, fill emptiness, or reward yourself after a hard day. These patterns make sense—food is available, comforting, and immediate. But when eating becomes your primary way to cope, it stops serving your Authentic Self.

Notice the beliefs underneath your eating patterns. Do you believe you don't deserve to enjoy food? That you must earn meals through exercise or productivity? That your worth is tied to your weight or what you eat? These beliefs belong to your Created Self, absorbed from family, diet culture, or painful experiences. Your Authentic Self knows that eating is a basic human need—not something to earn, restrict, or feel ashamed about.

Practical Mindful Eating

Mindful eating brings you back to the present moment and reconnects you with your body's wisdom.

- **Pause before eating.** Before your first bite, take a breath. Set an intention, offer gratitude, or simply notice that you're about to nourish yourself. This brief pause shifts you from autopilot to presence.
- **Notice hunger and fullness.** Ask yourself: Am I physically hungry, or am I eating for another reason? As you eat, check in

with your body. Fullness builds gradually—give yourself time to notice it.

- **Slow down.** Put your fork down between bites. Chew thoroughly. Taste the food rather than inhaling it. Eating slowly supports digestion and allows satisfaction to register before you've overeaten.
- **Minimize distractions.** When possible, eat without screens, work, or multitasking. Let the meal be its own experience rather than background activity.
- **Release judgment.** You ate something your Created Self labels "bad"? Notice the judgment and let it go. One meal doesn't define your health or your worth. Guilt doesn't improve nutrition—it only adds suffering.

WHEN PROFESSIONAL SUPPORT IS NEEDED

For some people, the relationship with food involves more than Created Self patterns. Eating disorders—including anorexia, bulimia, binge eating disorder, and others—are serious medical conditions that require professional treatment. If you experience obsessive thoughts about food or weight, engage in purging or severe restriction, feel out of control around eating, or notice that food dominates your mental and emotional life, please seek support from a healthcare provider or eating disorder specialist.

As you will learn in "Self-Care Tip: When to Seek Professional Help," recognizing when you need more than self-care is wisdom, not weakness. You deserve compassionate, specialized care.

FOOD AS SELF-CARE

In "Self-Care Tip: Make a Meal," you will explore preparing food as an act of love for your body. This article extends that invitation: let eating itself become self-care.

Your Authentic Self doesn't need you to eat perfectly. It needs you to eat with presence, compassion, and care. Some days that means a home-cooked meal savored slowly. Other days it means takeout eaten on the couch—without guilt. What matters is the relationship you bring to food, not the food itself.

You deserve to nourish yourself without shame. Your body deserves to be fed without judgment. Let meals become moments of care rather than tests you pass or fail.

Intention of the Day

I will approach one meal today with presence and compassion so that eating becomes care rather than conflict.

Self-Care Tip: Make a Meal

One of the love languages is acts of service. So show your body some love by preparing a meal for it. It does not have to be something big, fancy, or complicated. Even if you do not think of yourself as a cook, you can still do this. Preparing a meal can be as simple as assembling a salad of romaine lettuce with tomatoes and onions with a bit of olive oil and balsamic vinegar. Or it could be a ham and cheese sandwich with lettuce, sliced tomatoes, and red onions on whole wheat bread. Whether you take five minutes or an hour, what matters is that you are choosing to nourish yourself.

When you prepare your own food, you are making conscious choices about what goes into your body. You decide what ingredients to use and how much of each one. You choose foods that appeal to you, that make you feel good, or that meet your body's needs in that moment. This is not about perfection or following rules. It is about taking care of yourself with intention.

Preparing food also gives you space for creative expression. You can experiment with flavors by adding herbs or spices you enjoy. You can arrange food on the plate in a way that looks appealing to you. You can try a new combination you have been curious about. Even small creative choices, like adding fresh basil to a sandwich or drizzling honey on yogurt, make the experience more personal and satisfying.

When you finish preparing your meal, take a moment to appreciate what you have done. You chose to care for yourself. You took time to create something nourishing. That is an achievement worth recognizing, no matter how simple the meal.

Have fun with food today!

Self-Care Tip: Have a Hot Bath

Want to learn about a self-care practice that can reduce stress, relax tight muscles, and improve your sleep? Take a bath.

Warm water does more than clean your body. It relaxes your muscles by increasing blood flow and reducing tension. The heat helps your nervous system shift from stress to rest, which is why a bath before bed improves sleep. Taking time in the bath allows your mind to slow down and let go of the day's stress.

I have a very tight lower back, and a hot bath is one of the few ways to get it to relax. I add Epsom salts and Dead Sea salt to the water. After about ten minutes, I can feel my muscles letting go and the space between my vertebrae increase. Such a relief.

A bath is one of the most flexible forms of self-care. You can make it simple with plain warm water, or create a spa-like experience with a bath pillow, music, and candlelight. The water temperature can range from lukewarm to a safe one hundred four degrees Fahrenheit. Whether for ten minutes or thirty minutes, a bath gives your mind and body the care they deserve.

You can add Epsom salts to reduce joint swelling. Dead Sea salt helps cleanse and soothe irritated skin. Essential oils can either energize or calm you, depending on what you choose. You decide what your bath includes based on what you need. What you do during your bath also matters. If your mind needs quiet, lie in the tub in peaceful rest or meditation. If you need distraction from stress or pain, watch a show on your water-resistant smartphone. If you want connection, call someone you care about. Different activities serve different needs, and all are valid.

When you finish, take your time getting out. Warm water can make you lightheaded, and wet surfaces are slippery. Move slowly and steady yourself as needed. Have a nice bath!

Self-Care Tip: Aromatherapy

Aromatherapy is the use of plant extracts called essential oils to support your health and mood. These oils come from the roots, leaves, bark, flowers, or fruit peels of plants. Research shows that some essential oils have antimicrobial activity in lab studies (meaning they may slow the growth of germs). Gentle reminder: This book offers supportive self-care tools and is not a substitute for medical or mental health care.

Across history, people have turned to plants for support—through teas, herbs, aromatic resins, and oils. While essential oils are not a substitute for medical care, they can be a beautiful part of holistic self-care through scent, ritual, and nervous system support.

You have probably been benefiting from essential oils without realizing it. Vicks VapoRub contains camphor, eucalyptus, peppermint, cedar leaf, and nutmeg. Listerine uses thyme, peppermint, wintergreen, and eucalyptus. These familiar products include essential oils, which is part of what gives them their signature scent and effect.

Essential oils can help with focus, stress relief, and better sleep. Some people also use them to support skin comfort and soothing self-care rituals. My favorite ways to use them include a eucalyptus-lavender bed linen spray that helps me fall asleep faster. I enjoy diffusing eucalyptus, peppermint, lemon, and lime when I want my space to feel fresh and clear. Many people find these essential oils supportive for breathing comfort and mental clarity. I make a body butter with pink grapefruit oil that feels uplifting and refreshing.

You can buy essential oils at grocery stores, drugstores, local farms, or online. Books, workshops, and classes can teach you how to use them safely and make your own products.

Essential oils are powerful and need careful use. Some oils can cause skin irritation or burns if not diluted properly. They can trigger allergic reactions. Certain oils should be avoided during pregnancy. Some are toxic to pets. Always research an essential oil before using it and follow safety guidelines. Essential oils are not a substitute for medical care.

Treat yourself to aromatherapy today and discover what works for you.

Self-Care Tip: Weighted Blankets

With our fast-paced, mind-cluttering existence, stress, anxiety, and lack of restful sleep are very common among adults. One tool for helping ease these issues is the weighted blanket.

I never used to fall asleep while watching TV. I'm a person who does not fall asleep anywhere other than in a bed unless I am sick. But when I was going through a very stressful time and struggling with sleep, I heard that weighted blankets were helpful for people with PTSD, particularly veterans. I decided to give one a try. I bought a fifteen-pound weighted blanket about the size of a throw. I tried it out while watching TV. I fell asleep ten minutes in. Since then, I can't live without a weighted blanket. I now have four—one for winter, two for summer, and that original throw for watching TV.

Weighted blankets were originally created in the 1990s to provide calming effects for those with mental health conditions. They apply "deep touch pressure" to the body, which provides feedback to our nervous system that reduces anxiety and makes it easier to fall asleep, similar to swaddling a baby.

Weighted blankets come in various sizes and weights. The recommended weight for sleeping is about ten percent of your body weight. If that feels too heavy, it's fine to go lighter. Some are puffy like a comforter for warmth. Others are thin to provide breathability for people who have night sweats. For those who need help managing stress and anxiety during the day, lap blankets and throws are great to use while seated at a desk, traveling, or lounging on the couch.

Weighted blankets are available for both adults and children who weigh at least fifty pounds. They can be easily purchased online or in department stores. So curl up with one for more calm, a better night's sleep, and a cozy hug on demand.

Self-Care Tip: Sleep Hygiene

Sleep is the foundation of all other self-care. Without quality rest, your body has a harder time recovering, your mind has a harder time processing emotions, and your energy can drop. You can meditate, eat well, and exercise daily—but if your sleep suffers, everything else becomes harder.

Sleep hygiene refers to the habits and environment that support restful sleep. Think of it as preparing for sleep, not just falling into it.

I've learned that different sleep disruptions need different solutions. When my mind is busy, Solfeggio sleep music helps quiet the chatter. When I've sat at the computer all day, five minutes of stretching before bed releases the tension. After a very stressful day, lavender and chamomile tea helps me feel calmer. I also discovered that some changes take two to three days to show results—like when I extended my wind-down time to a full hour. Patience matters.

YOUR WAKE-UP ROUTINE (ABOUT ONE HOUR)

How you start the day affects how you sleep that night. Give yourself at least one hour before rushing into obligations.

- **Wash your face and brush your teeth.** These simple acts signal to your body that a new day has begun.
- **Drink water.** Your body has been without hydration for hours. A full glass of water supports your organs and energy.
- **Have breakfast and give yourself at least thirty minutes for digestion.** Rushing or skipping meals can make your body feel stressed.
- **Get sun exposure for at least ten minutes.** Open all your window blinds and curtains. Natural light supports your internal clock and helps your brain wake up.
- **Stretch.** Gentle movement wakes up your muscles and releases any stiffness from sleep.

DURING THE DAY

- Aim for a consistent sleep schedule when you can, even on weekends. Your body thrives on rhythm.
- If you work varying shifts, adjust other activities to stay as close to your regular sleep time as possible. Consistency matters more than perfection.

TWO TO THREE HOURS BEFORE BED

Try to finish large meals. This can help reduce discomfort and heartburn.

ONE TO TWO HOURS BEFORE BED

Limit large amounts of fluids. If you wake up to use the bathroom often, this may help.

YOUR WIND-DOWN ROUTINE (AT LEAST ONE HOUR)

This hour is sacred. It tells your body and mind that sleep is coming.

- **Limit screens if you can.** Blue light and scrolling can keep your brain alert. If you need a screen, dim it, use night mode, and consider blue light blocking glasses.

- **Shower or bathe.** Beyond relaxation, this removes dirt, dust, and pollen so they don't accumulate on your bedding and bother allergies.
- **Engage in calming activities.** Gentle stretching, journaling, or quiet conversation. Whatever helps your mind settle.

Your Bedroom Environment

- **Adjust the temperature.** Your bedroom should be slightly cooler than what's comfortable during the day. A cool environment supports deeper sleep.
- **Check your mattress and pillow.** Replace them as recommended by the manufacturer. In between replacements, rotate or flip your mattress at least twice a year to maintain support.
- **Consider your pets.** If a pet disturbs your sleep by moving, making noise, or waking you for attention, they may need to sleep outside the bedroom. This can be a hard boundary to set—and it's worth it.

Sleep Aids to Explore

Gentle reminder: This book offers supportive self-care tools and is not a substitute for medical or mental health care.

When you need extra support, these tools can help:

- **Teas.** Lavender and chamomile are naturally calming.
- **Supplements.** Some people explore supplements like melatonin or magnesium glycinate as part of their sleep routine. Always research them first, and check with your healthcare provider if you are pregnant, take medication, or have a health condition.
- **Sound.** White or brown noise machines block disruptive sounds. Some people enjoy Solfeggio sleep music to help the mind slow down.
- **Weighted blankets.** As you learned in "Self-Care Tip: Weighted Blankets," the gentle pressure provides a calming effect that helps many people fall asleep faster.

- **Sleep stories.** Apps like Calm offer narrated stories designed to ease you into sleep.

Your Authentic Self knows that rest isn't optional—it's essential. When you honor your sleep, you give every other dimension of your health a stronger foundation.

Be a Bum

Seriously. As an adult, you always have something that needs to get done. Always. Cleaning, cooking, gardening, laundry, work, return phone calls, check email, post on social media, grocery shopping, put gas in the car...

Enough.

Relax. I mean it. It's time to chill. I don't mean go on vacation, because that means you'd have to pack and travel. No. Relax. Be a bum for one day. No obligations of any sort, of any kind beyond the basic requirements for animal survival: eat, sleep, pee, poop, and breathe. That's it.

It may seem impossible, but humans discovered fire, flight, and the atomic bomb. You are more than capable of creating one day of complete rest.

When I take a Bum Day, I don't even check the mail. I stay in pajamas if I want. I read, nap, watch TV, stare at the ceiling—whatever my body and mind need without any agenda. And here's the key: I set boundaries to protect it.

When I tell people I'm taking a Bum Day, someone always calls asking if I want to go out and do something. I say no, I'm busy. They protest: "But it's your Bum Day. You have nothing to do." I reply: "Exactly. I'm busy being a bum." Your Bum Day is an appointment with yourself. Guard it like you would any other important commitment.

Your Authentic Self knows that rest isn't laziness—it's essential. But your Created Self, trained to earn your worth through productivity, will protest. Ignore it. Pick one day next month to have absolutely nothing to do other than what you want to do for you. Start planning for that day now. Your mind, body, and spirit will thank you for the opportunity to just be. Plus, you'll be surprised at how much more energy and focus you have the next day.

Intention of the Day
I will protect one day this month to be a complete bum.

Indulge Yourself

Today, think about what brings you happiness.
- Is it independence, achievement, or taking care of others?
- Does seeing life through an objective lens give you confidence?
- Does having a sense of belonging fill you with gratitude?

Whatever it is that grants you moments of peace and positivity, do you have access to it? Do you even know what it is?

Each time we indulge in the things that feed the soul, we strengthen our ability to navigate all that life throws at us. We fill up our tanks and charge our batteries so that we can keep going—physically, mentally, emotionally, and spiritually. How else are we going to keep negative energy from draining us dry?

Here's what I want you to do: make a list of the things that make you happy. It doesn't matter how long the list is. My list includes playing with dogs and cats (my friends' or at the local shelter), crystals, sleep, watching TV and movies, listening to music, taking care of my rose plants, knitting and crocheting, exploring my local area, and going out to eat with my friends. Once you have your list, post it somewhere in plain sight—a note on the refrigerator door, a dry erase board in your home office, wherever you'll see it daily. Then, over the next two weeks, carve out time for each item on your list. Even fifteen minutes counts. The goal is to actively engage with the things that bring you joy.

When you intentionally make space for happiness, you create an environment where peace and positivity can thrive.

Intention of the Day
I will make a list of what brings me joy and schedule time for it.

Understanding Overindulgence

You may ask yourself, "Why can't I stop overspending, overeating, or overdoing whatever brings temporary relief?" You know better. You understand the consequences. Yet you keep reaching for that quick fix. What's really happening?

The reason you can't seem to stop overindulging is that you're burnt out. Think of it like dehydration. When you don't drink enough water for days, your body triggers hunger to extract water from food. You eat more, but you're still thirsty because food wasn't what you actually needed. Burnout works the same way. When you are tired, stressed, and drained from daily obligations, your mind searches for the easiest path to feeling good. It reaches for spending money, extra servings, or another episode—not because these things truly give you joy, comfort, safety, or love, but because they're quick and available.

Treating yourself brings genuine positive emotions. Overindulging is your exhausted mind grasping for those same emotions through the fastest route possible. Just as drinking water satisfies your body and stops false hunger, finding authentic ways to experience positive emotions satisfies your mind and reduces the urge to overdo it. This might mean a fifteen-minute walk outside for fresh air and movement. Or journaling for ten minutes to process what's weighing on you. Or something else entirely that speaks to your needs. These kinds of activities provide the joy, comfort, or connection you're seeking without the guilt that follows overindulgence—your Authentic Self knows which ones truly nourish you.

I know this seems impossible when you're juggling work, caring for others, and trying to keep up with the world around you. But finding small moments for self-care that genuinely gives you positive emotions is the key to breaking the cycle. Your Authentic Self knows the difference between what truly nourishes and what only numbs.

Intention of the Day
I will find authentic ways to experience the positive emotions I'm seeking.

Breaking the Overindulgence Cycle

The urge to overindulge can feel overwhelming in the moment. You know you shouldn't, but the pull is strong. Here's a simple technique that gives you space between impulse and action: Delay-Distract-Decide, also known as the "3 Ds."

When you recognize the urge to overindulge, delay acting on it for at least thirty minutes. During that time, pick a task with a clear beginning and end—something you can complete and see the results of. Fold a load of laundry. Organize one drawer. Take a short walk around your neighborhood. Water your plants and wipe down their leaves. Spend ten minutes sketching or coloring.

The key is choosing an activity you can finish within that thirty-minute window. Once you complete it, decide whether you still need to overindulge.

This technique works because accomplishing something tangible—even small—triggers a release of dopamine in your brain. That's the same feel-good chemical you were chasing through overindulgence. When you finish folding the laundry or clearing that drawer, you get an instant reward: visible progress and a sense of achievement. This positive feeling reinforces the habit of choosing productive tasks instead of overindulgence.

The pause also allows the initial urge to settle. Often, you'll discover the impulse has passed or significantly weakened.

Even though the drive to overdo it seems impossible to resist, recognizing it and taking one intentional pause is your biggest step toward freedom. You're building a new pattern, one thirty-minute window at a time.

Intention of the Day
I will pause before overindulging so I can choose what truly serves me.

Self-Care Tip: Meditate

Meditation works. Whether it's for three minutes or forty minutes, meditation helps your mind and body settle down. Whether you are feeling anxious about an upcoming meeting, have a headache, or have trouble falling asleep, meditation can help. The process doesn't have to be a big to-do where you need special clothes, equipment, teas, and incense. It can be as simple as sitting at your desk at work with your eyes closed while taking a few gentle deep breaths at your own pace for a couple minutes.

You can meditate practically anywhere, even while sitting at a gate in a crowded airport. If you don't feel comfortable closing your eyes, you can still meditate. Pick an object to look at. Spend one minute slowly looking at every part of it. Notice its colors, shape, texture, and shadows.

There are many types of meditation, but here are a few you can explore to start:

- **Breathing meditation:** Focus on your breath moving in and out of your body.

- **Guided meditation:** Follow along with a recorded voice that guides you to relax and imagine peaceful scenes.
- **Sitting meditation:** Sit quietly and observe your thoughts without judgment.
- **Walking meditation:** Move slowly and mindfully, paying attention to each step.

Don't worry if your mind wanders during meditation—that's completely normal. The practice isn't about stopping all thoughts. It's about noticing when your mind drifts and gently bringing your attention back. If you are new to meditation, there are YouTube videos and apps such as Headspace and Calm that can guide you in different ways. You can also check out local meditation classes, meeting groups, and retreats.

So, whether you are extremely busy or bored out of your mind, meditate a bit each day. If you stick with it long enough, it will be a game changer for getting better sleep, taming the mind chatter, and giving you an energy boost for getting through your day!

Clear the Mental Backlog

Think of meditation as a process of catching up on the backlog of thoughts, feelings, and emotions in your brain.

When you experience the monkey mind (mind chatter), it's like having a backlog of inventory (information) in a warehouse (the mind) that you haven't had a chance to sort away on shelves. There is also a long line of trucks outside waiting to bring in more inventory. Meditation is the act of intentionally not accepting any new inventory so that you can catch up on sorting and putting away your current inventory in the warehouse. Translation: Meditation is the act of not taking in any new information so that your thoughts, feelings, and emotions can be fully sorted through and released.

When you are still, either in quiet, while listening to music, or while listening to a guided meditation, that is the act of not bringing in information from the world around you. Sometimes, doing tasks such as going for a walk, washing dishes, or knitting can be used as meditation because you are not taking in more information during those activities. When you have mind chatter while being still, that's actually the mind sorting through the backlog of thoughts that were never completed, feelings that were never fully felt, and emotions that were never thoroughly expressed. When you have finally sorted through that backlog, your mind becomes quiet and you experience what it truly means to be present.

So, it is completely normal to be thinking a lot when you start a meditation routine. What is most important is taking the time to meditate regularly. That way you can eventually catch up on the backlog of your thoughts, feelings, and emotions and become present.

Intention of the Day
I will give my mind time and space to catch up to the present moment.

Silence is Golden

If you've ever had trouble falling asleep because your mind chatter is going a mile a minute, I'm sure you'd agree that silence is golden.

I bought my 2011 Ford Focus in 2013. When I first drove it, I liked that the engine had a little growl to it. Over three years, that growl gradually got louder and the car vibrated more. Eventually, it got so loud I could barely hear myself think. When I finally took it to the mechanic and got it fixed, the quiet startled me. I could barely hear the engine running. It took several drives to adjust. But once I did, I realized how much calmer my mind and body felt without all that noise.

Your mind works the same way. You get so used to constant mental noise that you don't realize how much it's wearing you down. With information constantly coming at you from TV, internet, radio, and books from the moment you wake up to when you go to bed, your mind is always thinking and processing. It seems hard to shut down. You may not even remember how to shut down. A lot of the exhaustion you feel as an adult is mental exhaustion. So now more than ever, you need to help your mind truly relax and restore. One of the best ways to do that is with silence.

Today, let's find room to just sit in silence, whether it's for five, three, or one minute at a time. Find a place where you can be alone, even if it means going for a walk or sitting in the bathroom. Just take time away from people and electronics and be in silence. Your mind may still chat away, but that's because it doesn't remember what to do with silence. If you practice often enough, the mind will start to learn to be silent. Then, that's when the "golden" part begins to kick in.

Intention of the Day
I will take time to be still in silence and give my mind some time off.

Self-Care Tip: Digital Wellness

Technology is woven into modern life. It connects us, informs us, and helps us work. But without mindful boundaries, it can also drain us. Screen fatigue is real. The pull to check, scroll, and respond is constant—and it's not your fault. These tools are designed to capture your attention. Reclaiming it is essential self-care.

I've felt this in my own body. The more often I scroll on my phone, the more my neck hurts. The more frequent the notification sounds, the more short-tempered I become—even if I don't check what the notification is for. My concentration fractures. Tasks that should take thirty minutes stretch into hours. And when I use my phone to keep up with the news without limits, I spend most of the day in a state of worry.

I've learned that digital wellness requires intention. Here's what works for me and what might work for you.

TAME YOUR NOTIFICATIONS

Not every ping deserves your attention. Go through your phone settings and turn off non-essential notifications. Keep only what truly matters—messages from loved ones, calendar reminders, urgent work communications. Every notification you eliminate is one less interruption pulling you out of the present moment.

CREATE PHONE-FREE ZONES AND TIMES

Some spaces and moments deserve your full presence. Consider keeping your phone away from meals, out of the bedroom, and untouched for the first hour after you wake. These boundaries protect your relationships, your sleep, and your morning peace. As you learned in "Self-Care Tip: Sleep Hygiene," screens before bed disrupt your rest. The same principle applies throughout your day—strategic separation supports your well-being.

BE INTENTIONAL WITH SOCIAL MEDIA

I'm very particular about what I use each platform for. Facebook is for keeping up with friends and family. LinkedIn is for job searches and connecting with industry colleagues. Instagram is for laughs, DIY inspiration, and inspirational messages. X is only for promoting my business. If anything shows up in my feeds outside of that purpose, I hide it or block it. Eventually, the algorithms catch on.

This clarity protects my energy. Social media becomes a tool I use rather than a void I fall into.

SET LIMITS ON CONSUMPTION

I spend no more than twenty minutes a day on social media. I watch TV no more than two hours on weekdays and four hours on weekend days. These aren't rigid rules—they're guardrails that keep entertainment from consuming time meant for other things.

Most smartphones have built-in screen time tracking. Use it. Not to judge yourself, but to see clearly. Awareness often motivates change without any additional effort.

MANAGE NEWS INTAKE

Staying informed matters. Drowning in headlines doesn't. I have one local news app and one national news app, both set to alert me only to top stories. I keep a separate weather app so I can check the forecast without stumbling into distracting news stories. This structure lets me stay aware without spending my day in worry.

PROTECT YOUR EYES AND BODY

Screens strain more than your attention. If you work at a computer, practice the 20-20-20 rule: every twenty minutes, look at something twenty feet away for twenty seconds. This simple habit reduces eye strain and gives your mind a micro-break.

Notice your posture too. Scrolling often means hunching. If your neck, shoulders, or back ache, your body is telling you something. Stretch, adjust your position, or step away entirely.

MINDFUL CONSUMPTION VS. MINDLESS SCROLLING

There's a difference between choosing to watch a show you enjoy and opening an app out of habit with no intention. Before you pick up your phone or turn on a screen, pause. Ask yourself: What am I looking for? Is this serving me right now?

Sometimes the answer is yes—you need a laugh, a distraction, or connection with a friend. Sometimes the answer is no—you're avoiding something, filling silence, or numbing discomfort. Both answers are okay. What matters is that you're choosing consciously.

As you learned in "Silence is Golden," our minds need rest from constant input. Digital boundaries create space for that silence—and for your Authentic Self to be heard.

START WITH ONE CHANGE

You don't have to overhaul your digital life today. Pick one boundary that feels manageable. Turn off one category of notifications. Keep your phone out of the bedroom for a week. Set a twenty-minute timer before opening social media. Small changes compound into freedom.

Technology should serve your life, not consume it. Your attention is precious. Protect it like the resource it is.

Self-Care Tip: Journaling

Like meditation, journaling is another tool that helps clear the backlog of thoughts, reduce mind chatter, and free up mental energy. Journaling can help you:

- **Remember tasks:** Reduces the need for your brain to constantly track what you need to do.
- **Take stock:** Understand what already is so you can see clearly what to do next.
- **Release what no longer serves you:** Write down unwanted thoughts, feelings, and emotions, then burn or rip up the paper as a way of letting them go.
- **Organize thoughts:** When your mind jumps between ideas, writing them down helps you focus on one at a time.

TYPES OF JOURNALING TO EXPLORE:

- **Self-love journaling:** Write down things you like about yourself, whether appearance, talents, accomplishments, or personality. It's easy to beat ourselves up and forget what we can celebrate.
- **Automatic writing:** Pick a topic and write whatever comes to mind about it. Great for problem-solving and generating ideas. This process helped me write this book.
- **Brain dumping:** Write down whatever pops into your head, even if it doesn't make sense. I've discovered patterns in my

thoughts this way, showing which topics or issues were taking up the most mental space.

- **Gratitude journaling:** List things you're grateful for each day. This can shift your thoughts and feelings from negative to positive, converting hopelessness to hope when you remember what you have to be grateful for, big and small.

HOW TO JOURNAL:

You can journal in a notebook or on your computer, tablet, or smartphone. You can write paragraphs or bulleted lists. You can even record audio journals. Try different formats and types to discover what works best for you.

DAILY JOURNALING PROMPTS:

<table>
<tr><td colspan="1">Date:</td></tr>
<tr><td>I am grateful for:

    1.

    2.

    3.

</td></tr>
<tr><td>I appreciate this about myself:

    1.

    2.

    3.

</td></tr>
<tr><td>Today's priorities:

    1.

    2.

    3.

</td></tr>
</table>

Free writing space (brain dump, automatic writing, or whatever you need today):

Understand Your Energy Body

Growing up, you learned to care for your physical body. You learned to bathe, brush your teeth, comb your hair, and drink water. But what do you know about your energy body?

The energy body is a subtle energetic system that mirrors your physical body. Many spiritual traditions teach that every living creature has one. It interacts with the energy around you—taking in what supports you and helping you release what doesn't. Your energy body also carries your thoughts, feelings, and emotions outward—whether you speak them or not.

Like the physical body, the energy body can be understood in many ways. Depending on the tradition, you may hear about the aura, chakras, or meridians. Most people cannot see this system with the naked eye. Some aspects of the human system can be measured, and some can only be experienced. SQUID-based technology can detect subtle magnetic fields produced by the body, including those associated with the heart and brain—something used in magnetoencephalography (MEG). That doesn't 'prove' everything we experience spiritually, but it does support a truth many of us feel deep down: we are more than just flesh and bone. Even though you may not see the energy body, you can feel it. Have you ever sensed someone behind you without hearing a sound? Many people experience this as an energetic awareness—your system picking up on another presence before your mind can explain it.

Why is it important to learn about this system? Because it can influence how you experience your physical body, your emotions, and your overall sense of wellbeing. Have you ever walked into a room where everyone is upset and immediately felt uncomfortable? A strong and supported energy body can help you stay grounded around other people's emotions. This allows you to be compassionate and aware without absorbing what doesn't belong to you.

How do you take care of your energy body? One way is by taking care of your physical form. The energy body affects the physical body, and the reverse is also true. Eating well, drinking water, and exercising benefit both systems. If you notice that you are easily affected by the "vibe" of other people or places, try to take care of your physical body. This can strengthen your energy body and improve how you move through different environments and energies.

Intention of the Day
I will care for my energy body so that it can support my whole health.

Self-Care Tip: Ground & Center

Feeling panicky, scattered, exhausted, or vulnerable? Grounding and centering can help. Though often mentioned together, they serve different purposes.

Grounding creates stability and connection. It anchors you to the present moment and to the Earth beneath you. When you're grounded, you feel steady and supported—less likely to be swept away by stress or overwhelm.

Centering brings you back to your core. It quiets mental noise and returns you to a calm, relaxed state where your Authentic Self can be heard. When you're centered, you think more clearly and trust your intuition.

Together, grounding and centering restore your inner strength. They help with focus, creativity, and navigating overwhelming situations. The key is having techniques ready before you need them.

QUICK TECHNIQUE: BREATHWORK (30 SECONDS)

When stress hits suddenly—at work, in traffic, before a difficult conversation—try this. Close your eyes if you can. Inhale slowly and imagine healing energy flowing in through the top of your head. As you exhale, imagine negative or stagnant energy releasing out through your feet and into the Earth. Repeat for three to five breaths. This simple practice can shift your state in under a minute.

BODY SCAN (2–3 MINUTES)

When you have a bit more time, try a body scan. Sit or lie comfortably and close your eyes. Starting at the top of your head, slowly move your attention downward through your body. Notice your forehead, jaw, neck, shoulders, arms, hands, chest, belly, hips, legs, and feet. Linger on each area for ten to fifteen seconds so you can fully sense it. Don't try to fix any tension—just notice it. This practice brings you into your body and out of racing thoughts.

GUIDED MEDITATION: LIGHT AND ROOTS (5–10 MINUTES)

For deeper grounding and centering, set aside time for this meditation. You can read through it first and then practice from memory, or record yourself reading it aloud and play it back.

Close your eyes and take a few deep, gentle breaths at your own pace.

Imagine you are gazing up into the sky and you see beautiful white clouds. As you gaze upward, a beautiful beam of light begins to shine down through the clouds.

The light shines down onto you, flowing through the top of your head. It moves down through your forehead, your eyes, throughout your sinuses, ears, nose, and lips. It flows throughout your mouth and down through your throat.

The light continues through your collarbones and shoulders, your upper arms, your elbows, and down through your lower arms, wrists, and hands. It also flows down throughout your chest, into your heart space, into your belly, and down into your pelvis. See this light flow through your hips, your thighs, your knees, down your lower legs, through your ankles, and down to the bottoms of your feet.

The bottoms of your feet are firmly on the ground, connected to the Earth. Imagine roots growing from the bottoms of your feet deep into the Earth. These roots continue downward until they meet the liquid core of the Earth. When the roots meet the Earth's core, the energy of the Earth flows up through your feet and legs, up through your belly, into your chest, up through your throat, and to the top of your head.

The light from above and the light of the Earth fill your body. Your body is stable, centered, and grounded upon the Earth.

Take as long as you like to enjoy the energies flowing through you. When you are ready, bring your attention to the touch of your body on the surface supporting you. Bring your awareness to your eyes, and then slowly open them and come back.

The audio versions of these practices are available at
https://www.mywealthinhealth.com/abundantly-you.html

Self-Care Tip: Get Your Energy Flowing

You learned about your energy body. Now let's explore how energy flows through it.

We get energy from the food we eat, and we need energy to get through the day. But there's another kind of energy at work. Traditional Chinese medicine teaches that just as blood flows through blood vessels, life energy flows throughout the body through pathways called meridians. Meridians are a network of channels connecting all parts of the body, delivering energy to where it's needed.

In this tradition, when the flow of energy feels stuck or heavy, you may feel tense, tired, or uncomfortable. Stress, hard experiences, and poor physical care can also affect how supported you feel in your body. *Gentle reminder:* This book offers supportive self-care tools and is not a substitute for medical or mental health care.

To support healthy energy flow, many people explore tools such as:

- **Acupuncture, acupressure, or reflexology:** Inserting needles into or applying pressure to points on the body to break up energy blocks.
- **Qigong or Tai chi:** Using physical movements to help move energy throughout the body.
- **Reiki:** A gentle healing practice that supports relaxation, energy balance, and inner peace.
- **Crystal healing:** Wearing crystals or placing them in your space to support energy balance and flow.
- **Sound therapy:** Using tuning forks, singing bowls, or sound recordings to shift energy and promote healing.

You can find practitioners for acupuncture, Reiki, and sound therapy through online directories or local wellness centers. Qigong and Tai chi classes are often offered at community centers, yoga studios, or parks. Crystals can be purchased at metaphysical shops or online. Sound therapy recordings are available on YouTube and meditation apps.

Try what resonates and notice what helps you feel more open, steady, and energized. If you are dealing with severe or ongoing symptoms, please seek medical support as well.

Self-Care Tip: Declutter Your Space

Your physical space reflects your mental state. When life feels chaotic, clutter accumulates. When your mind is overwhelmed, maintaining order becomes exhausting. This connection works both ways—clutter in your environment adds to mental clutter, making it harder to think clearly, find what you need, and feel at peace.

I've noticed this pattern in my own life. The more stressed I become, the more cluttered my home gets—and the clutter shows up in specific places. When my IBS and gastritis flare up, my kitchen and dining area fall into disarray. When work overwhelms me, my desk and home office collect piles. The external mess mirrors the internal struggle.

Sometimes we hold onto things because of who we think we should be rather than who we are. Boxes of craft supplies for hobbies you no longer enjoy. Books you'll never read but feel you ought to keep. Clothes that don't fit the life you're actually living. Letting go of these items isn't failure—it's honoring your Authentic Self.

Start small. Pick one drawer, one shelf, one corner. You can work alone or ask for help. Notice which areas accumulate clutter—they may reveal where stress is hiding.

Sometimes the issue isn't too much stuff but too little space. If your home still feels cluttered after you've let go of what you can, consider hiring a professional organizer or exploring Feng Shui—an ancient Chinese practice of arranging spaces to promote positive energy flow. Both can help you arrange what you have in ways that create calm instead of chaos. As you clear physical space, you create room for mental clarity.

Self-Care Tip: Affirmations

Affirmations are positive statements you speak or write to shift your mindset and reinforce what you value. They work by redirecting your thoughts away from criticism and toward compassion. When you repeat an affirmation regularly, it helps rewire how you think about yourself and the world around you.

You can use affirmations any time you need grounding, encouragement, or a gentle reminder of your worth. Say them aloud in the morning to set your intention for the day. Write them in your journal when processing difficult emotions. Repeat them silently during meditation or stressful moments. There is no wrong way to use them.

Here are some affirmations to support different aspects of your self-care journey:

BODY & PHYSICAL CARE

- I forgive every judgment of my body and accept my body just as it is.
- I honor nature's decision to energize, sustain, and reaffirm my existence through the food I eat.
- I choose a pace that is right for me.

MIND & EMOTIONAL WELLBEING

- My mind is free of judgment, even of myself.
- I give my hyper-vigilant mind the day off and trust that I am safe.
- I let go of negative thoughts to make room for joy, peace, and love.

RELATIONSHIPS & CONNECTION

- Being kind to myself is the first step to being kind to others.
- I accept others as they are to better understand them and myself.
- I am direct and honest in my communication with others.

PRESENT MOMENT & PEACE

- I place all my attention in the present moment.
- When I laugh, it is my soul saying, "All is well, and all will be well." I will then say, "Thank you for reminding me."
- I know peace, calm, and safety in the midst of uncertainty.

Choose one affirmation that speaks to what you need right now. Let it guide you today.

Section 2: Your Beliefs

Examine and choose what you believe

Listen to Your Intuition

Have you ever had a feeling about someone or something that you couldn't explain? No logical reason, no concrete evidence—just a knowing deep inside? That's your intuition speaking. You don't know how you know, but you just know it.

Intuition is your Authentic Self communicating with you. It's the voice beneath all the conditioning, the knowing that exists independent of what you've been taught or what others expect.

The problem is that most of us have been taught to ignore it. From childhood, we learn to rely only on facts and logic. Be nice. Don't judge people. Don't be "rude" by trusting a bad feeling about someone. Your Created Self learned to override your intuitive knowing to keep peace and meet expectations.

How many times have you met someone who seemed nice and polite, but you got the feeling to stay far away from them? You ignored it. Then weeks later, that person backstabbed you, lied to you, or humiliated you. Or you had a job interview that went well, but something felt off. You took the job anyway. Three months in, you had twice the workload promised, and the company culture was toxic.

You've had plenty of opportunities for your intuition to protect you. Now it's time to listen.

Intuition often feels calm and clear, even when delivering uncomfortable messages. It's different from anxiety or fear—it doesn't spiral or create worst-case scenarios. It simply knows. You don't need proof or evidence to trust it. The knowing itself is enough.

Life is short, and you don't have time for situations that drain you or people who harm you. Your Authentic Self is trying to guide you toward what serves you and away from what doesn't. Listen to your intuition, now more than ever.

Intention of the Day
I will listen to my intuition and trust what it tells me.

Understanding Where Your Beliefs Come From

Imagine you are preparing for a journey. Before you begin, your family and friends hand you a suitcase full of clothes. You pull it along, but it feels heavy. When you open it, you discover shirts printed with phrases like "Work Harder" and "Don't Be Too Loud." The jeans have "You Must Earn Your Rest" stitched into the fabric.

You didn't pack this suitcase. Your parents, teachers, and culture packed it for you. They weren't trying to hurt you—they believed they were giving you tools to survive. But they handed you a heavy collection of beliefs you never chose to carry.

Think of your beliefs like hand-me-down clothes. Throughout childhood, adults handed you beliefs to try on. "Good girls put everyone else first." "Asking for help shows weakness." "Your worth depends on what you produce." You didn't select these beliefs yourself. You simply adopted them because you were young and trusted the adults around you.

I carried an inherited belief for years without recognizing it. I assumed that single, childless people have more available time than married parents. Then I noticed how full my life actually was—caring for chosen family members, building a business, volunteering in my community. The belief didn't match my reality.

This realization reminded me of the word "spinster." Today it sounds like an insult directed at single, childless women. But historically, a spinster was the most valued person in a family—she made all the clothing when purchasing garments was too expensive. The negative meaning emerged because cultural attitudes shifted, not because single women themselves changed.

Your Authentic Self exists beneath these inherited beliefs. It didn't pack this suitcase. But now that you're an adult, you get to decide what stays and what goes.

Intention of the Day
I will notice one belief I hold and ask where it came from.

Inherited Beliefs vs. Chosen Beliefs

Sometimes you examine a belief in your suitcase and realize you want to keep it. The belief itself feels true to you. But the way your family or culture expects you to practice it feels heavy, stressful, or wrong.

Here is an important distinction: there is a difference between a belief and a practice. You can hold the same belief as your community while choosing to practice it in a way that honors your Authentic Self.

Take Christmas. I believe in the spirit of the holiday—a reflection of Christ's birth and a reminder of peace, belonging, and joy. But for years, I watched people turn it into a marathon of stress. The unspoken rules said Christmas meant buying impressive gifts, attending every party, and running yourself into exhaustion.

My Created Self tried to keep pace with that chaos. My Authentic Self asked: Does this actually make sense?

I decided to tailor the tradition to fit me. I still buy gifts for a handful of people, but I focus on meaningful rather than impressive—sometimes I make them instead. I decorate my home, mail cards, and call loved ones on Christmas Day. Same belief, completely different practice. I end the season feeling restored instead of depleted.

I hold a similar perspective on weddings. I believe the union belongs to the couple, the court, and whatever higher power they honor—not contingent on who attends. If wedding planning becomes overwhelming, couples should feel free to elope quietly, then hold the ceremony as a joyful celebration afterward. Friends of mine did exactly this, and their joy was evident. The outcome remained the same; the stress did not.

You have permission to do this with any belief in your suitcase. Honor your values while protecting your peace.

Intention of the Day
I will identify one belief I value and ask if my practice truly serves me.

Questioning Beliefs That No Longer Serve You

Now that you recognize your suitcase contains beliefs others packed for you, what comes next? You cannot simply wish them away. You have to actively sort through them, deciding what deserves to stay.

Here is a process you can use whenever you feel anxious, small, or inadequate. It's called the 3-Step Reality Check.

- **Step 1: Notice It.** Catch the belief and observe it with curiosity rather than judgment, naming what you're actually thinking: "I believe that leaving this situation means I'm a failure."
- **Step 2: Ask, "Is It True?"** Put the belief on trial by examining the evidence. What actually supports this belief? What contradicts it? Is it based on facts or on fear that was passed down to you?
- **Step 3: Ask, "Does It Help?"** Consider whether holding this belief makes you healthier, kinder to yourself, or more aligned with your Authentic Self. If the answer is no, you have permission to release it.

I used this process when deciding to leave my Ph.D. program. Throughout graduate school, I was told that people who leave would amount to nothing—that choosing industry over academia meant selling out. I believed this narrative for years.

Then I remembered a colleague who had dropped out. He went on to live a much happier life, doing meaningful work that helped others in a non-academic role. His journey contradicted everything I had been told. I recognized that if he could thrive after leaving, so could I. The belief wasn't true, and it certainly wasn't helping me.

When you release a belief, plant something new in its place—otherwise, the old thought pattern eventually returns. When I released "leaving means failure," I replaced it with "leaving means choosing myself." That new belief supported my Authentic Self instead of undermining it.

Your peace matters more than their expectations.

Intention of the Day
I will question one belief that makes me feel small and ask if it is true.

The "Should" Trap

If you want to catch your Created Self in action, listen for one word: should.

"I should be further along in my career by now." "I should say yes to that favor." "I should not feel this tired." "I should be able to handle this without help."

The word "should" is a warning light. It signals that you may be measuring yourself against someone else's expectations rather than your own truth. When that light flashes, pause and investigate.

Not every "should" points to an inherited belief. Sometimes "should" reflects genuine alignment with your values—"I should call my grandmother because connection matters to me." But often, "should" reveals pressure from outside sources: family expectations, cultural norms, or standards you absorbed without choosing them.

Here is a simple test. When you notice yourself thinking or saying "should," ask:

- Whose voice is this?
- Is this expectation something I consciously chose or something I inherited?
- Does meeting this expectation serve my Authentic Self, or does it serve only someone else's comfort?

If you discover the "should" comes from an inherited belief that no longer serves you, return to the 3-Step Reality Check from the previous article. Notice the belief, question whether it's true, and ask whether it helps you.

You can also shift your language to reveal what's really happening. Replace "should" with "could" or "choose to" and notice how the sentence feels different. "I should exercise more" carries obligation and judgment. "I could exercise more" opens possibility. "I choose to exercise because it supports my energy" reflects conscious decision. The shift from "should" to "choose" moves you from your Created Self back to your Authentic Self.

Pay attention to how often "should" appears in your thoughts this week. Each one is an invitation to investigate.

Intention of the Day
I will notice when I say "should" and ask whose expectation I am meeting.

Beliefs About Worthiness

The "shoulds" we explored in "The 'Should' Trap" often trace back to a deeper belief: that you must constantly prove your worth. The Created Self insists you are like a prepaid phone—you only have value if you have "minutes" left on your account. If you aren't producing, achieving, or helping, you are empty and therefore worthless.

This is the biggest lie of the Created Self: you have to earn your right to exist.

In graduate school, I absorbed this belief completely. Your worth as a scientist was measured by publications. During my first year, I proposed a solution to a problem a professor was struggling with. He dismissed my idea as garbage and told me I was wasting his time. Three years later, he published research based on that very idea—without acknowledging me.

I was furious for years. The people with power to help me refused because it didn't benefit them. But eventually, I recognized something important: my idea had made significant contributions to developmental biology and helped scientists around the world. My worth existed independent of whether my name appeared on that paper. The idea proved my value to society, even if that professor never acknowledged it.

Here is the truth your Authentic Self already knows: you do not have to earn your existence. Consider nature. Does a tree earn its sunlight? Does a cell apologize for taking up space? They belong simply because they exist. You are part of nature too. You are not a machine that must justify its presence through output.

Your worth is inherent. It was there before you achieved anything, and it remains even when you rest. The Created Self will keep demanding proof. Your Authentic Self knows no proof is required.

Intention of the Day
I will remind myself that my worth exists even when I am not producing.

Rest vs. Laziness

If you've ever felt guilty for sitting down, taking a nap, or doing nothing productive, you're not alone. Many of us carry a quiet shame around rest—a voice that whispers you should be doing more, working harder, earning your right to stop.

That voice isn't your Authentic Self. It's your Created Self, shaped by a culture that equates worth with productivity.

From childhood, you may have absorbed messages that rest is for the weak, the unmotivated, the lazy. You learned that good people stay busy. That taking a break means falling behind. That if you're not exhausted, you're not trying hard enough. These beliefs burrow deep, and they don't disappear just because you're tired. They make rest feel like failure.

But rest and laziness are not the same thing.

Rest is restorative. It replenishes your energy, repairs your body, and clears your mind. Rest is an intentional act of self-care that allows you to return to life with more capacity than before. Your Authentic Self knows when rest is needed—and honors that need without apology.

Laziness, on the other hand, is often avoidance. It's not about restoration but about escaping something—fear, overwhelm, depression, or tasks that feel too big to face. When you find yourself unable to move forward despite adequate rest, that's worth exploring with curiosity rather than judgment. Laziness often signals something deeper that deserves attention.

I learned this distinction during two and a half years of part-time work. I cobbled together contract positions and part-time jobs, none of which offered benefits. When I couldn't make enough money to meet my needs, I blamed myself. I felt I wasn't doing enough. So whenever I rested, guilt consumed me.

It took time to recognize the truth: no amount of work would have been sufficient. The pay rates, the lack of benefits, the economic conditions—these were systemic, not personal failures. My exhaustion was real. My need for rest was legitimate. The guilt was Created Self programming telling me I hadn't earned the right to stop.

As you explored in "Take a Break," your body sends clear signals when rest is needed. And as you discovered in "Be a Bum," complete rest—doing absolutely nothing—is essential self-care. The guilt you feel around rest isn't wisdom. It's conditioning. Your Authentic Self knows the difference between restoration and avoidance. Trust that knowing.

You don't have to earn rest through suffering. You don't have to justify rest through productivity. Rest is not a reward for exhaustion. It's a basic human need—and meeting it is never laziness.

Intention of the Day
I will rest without guilt today so that I honor what my body truly needs.

The Impossibility of Pleasing Everyone

In modern society, getting as many things done as quickly as possible has become a strict expectation. Multitasking and overachieving are now the measuring sticks for success and worthiness. We feel pressure to excel in others' eyes. In response, we sacrifice our health, time, money, and self-respect.

When chasing approval, we lose sight of our needs until we've sacrificed too much. I learned this the hard way. Relatives, teachers, and bosses would brag about my high performance to others—not because they were proud of me, but because I made them look good. When I was an undergraduate working in a lab, the professor told others I was the best undergraduate student he ever had. But he never praised me directly. He just criticized me.

The cost of overperforming for others' approval shows up everywhere: chronic health issues, debt, damaged relationships, double workloads. Does pursuing others' definitions of success warrant sacrificing your well-being? What's the point if you're too burned out to enjoy it?

Let's face facts. There are over eight billion people on Earth, and you will never make all of them happy. Even if you cared about only three people, you could not please them all. Happiness comes only from within. There are many tools and tips on becoming happy, but they don't make you happy by themselves.

Your Authentic Self knows this truth: you cannot pour from an empty cup. When you sacrifice your well-being to meet others' expectations, you're not serving anyone—not them and certainly not yourself. People who care about you want you healthy and happy. Those who only value what you can do for them aren't asking you to be your Authentic Self. They're asking you to be useful to them. So let's not go overboard chasing others' definition of success. Your well-being matters more than their approval.

Intention of the Day
I will take care of myself so that I am of use to myself.

Your Body Is Not the Problem

The beliefs you hold about your body—what it should weigh, how it should look, what it should be capable of—rarely come from your

Authentic Self. Most come from your Created Self, absorbing messages from family, culture, and media about what bodies are "supposed" to be.

These beliefs cause real harm. They tell you that your worth depends on your appearance. They insist your body is a problem to fix rather than a companion to honor. They demand you achieve standards that may be physically impossible given your actual circumstances.

I know this personally. I have endometriosis, which required synthetic progesterone treatment. I gained forty pounds in two months. My pre-existing knee problems worsened with the weight gain, reducing my physical activity and creating more weight gain. Even though I eat less than most people I know and exercise more, my weight has been a struggle. People who claim to care about me insist I eat too much, that I have "no excuse" for my body. My doctors say I'm healthy given my conditions. But others—even those closest to me—reject that truth and impose their own beliefs instead.

You might face similar judgment. Mobility issues, PCOS, endometriosis, menopause, chronic illness, or simply aging changes your body in ways others don't understand. They compare your body to unrealistic standards or to how you used to look. They act as if your body is a moral failing rather than a reality shaped by biology, medical conditions, and life itself.

Here's what your Authentic Self knows: your body is not the problem. The beliefs others project onto it are the problem.

Those beliefs come from Created Self programming—the idea that bodies must look a certain way to have value. Your family absorbed these beliefs from their culture. Media reinforces them daily. But they are not truth. They are inherited opinions dressed up as facts.

It's natural to grieve the body you once had. Maybe you were more mobile, had less pain, or fit cultural beauty standards more easily. That grief is valid. You can honor what you've lost while also appreciating what your body does for you now. Grieving and appreciation aren't opposites— they coexist.

Your body's worth isn't measured by how closely it matches someone else's idea of what it should be. Health looks different for everyone.

Beauty isn't one size, one shape, one age. Your Authentic Self knows this, even when others insist otherwise.

You get to redefine your relationship with your body on your own terms. That means caring for it rather than punishing it. It means trusting your doctors and your own lived experience over others' judgments. It means recognizing that aging and changing are natural—not failures.

As you will learn in "You Are Fine As You Are," the things others see as shortcomings might help someone else. As you will explore in "The Comparison Trap," your body has its own thresholds shaped by your unique biology and circumstances. No one else lives in your body. Their beliefs about it don't define its value.

Your body has carried you through every moment of your life. It deserves your respect—not because it looks a certain way, but because it's yours.

Intention of the Day
I will honor my body's truth today and release others' beliefs about what it should be.

The Comparison Trap

"**E**veryone else manages, why can't I?"
This thought feels so real when you're struggling while others seem fine. You watch your friend exercise daily while you can only manage three times a week. You see parents handling their children's demands without complaint while you feel exhausted just thinking about one more request. The comparison tells you something must be wrong with you.

Here's what that comparison misses: no two people on this planet have identical limits. Your Authentic Self knows this truth, even when your Created Self insists you should keep up with everyone else.

COMPARING YOUR CAPACITY

Two of the greatest obstacles to self-care are negative self-talk and comparing yourself to others. Just because parents are often tired doesn't mean they should never feel exhausted and need a break from their children. Just because you're expected to stay busy at work doesn't mean you can't have too much to handle. Just because your friend exercises every day doesn't make you lazy for exercising three times a week.

Your body, mind, and energy have their own thresholds—shaped by your biology, life experiences, current circumstances, and whatever else you're carrying. When you compare your capacity to someone else's, you're measuring yourself against a standard that was never meant for you.

COMPARING YOUR IDENTITY

The comparison trap goes deeper than capacity. Each culture has specific expectations for different groups. Men should be physically strong. Women should cook. Teenagers should get good grades in school. Children should be seen, not heard. The problem with having specific expectations for whole sections of society is that it's unrealistic.

It's unrealistic because we're each unique in biology and experiences. Even identical twins, who share the same DNA, develop different personalities and preferences. So why should you expect someone else to be just like you or you to be just like someone else? That belief tricks us into negative self-talk and weakens our confidence and self-esteem.

These cultural expectations shape your Created Self—the version of you trying to meet external standards. But your Authentic Self knows the truth: you don't need to match anyone's template to have value.

THE ROLE OF MENTORS

There's nothing wrong with having mentors, teachers, or role models. They help you discover what's meaningful to YOU and show different ways to achieve YOUR goals. But as unique individuals, we're each meant to travel our own path toward a fulfilling life. Mentors illuminate possibilities—they don't provide a blueprint you must copy. Traveling your own path means finding happiness within yourself and expressing yourself to the world in a way you can be proud of.

YOUR UNIQUE PLACE

Think of a five-thousand-piece jigsaw puzzle showing a beautiful landscape. No two pieces are identical, yet each one is essential to completing the picture. If pieces tried to be like other pieces instead of being themselves, the puzzle could never come together. The same is true for humanity. Your unique contribution is needed exactly as it is.

So if you're not the puzzle piece that becomes a professor, weighs one hundred twenty pounds, owns a mansion, or speaks a second language, no worries. The jigsaw puzzle of humanity is not complete without you.

Your Authentic Self doesn't need you to match anyone else's pace or path. It needs you to recognize your actual limits and honor them. Stay in your lane. Not because you're less capable, but because your lane is the only one designed for your journey.

Intention of the Day
I will honor my limits today without comparing them to anyone else's capacity.

Spirituality and Your Authentic Self

When discussing beliefs, we eventually arrive at the big one: religion. For some people, religion is a source of comfort. For others, it carries guilt. And for some, it is simply something they do because their family did it. But in the search for your Authentic Self, it helps to understand the difference between religion and spirituality.

Religion is a set of maps, rituals, and rules passed down by a community. It is a guidepost. Spirituality is the actual journey—the practice of connecting with your own heart and with something bigger than yourself. You can memorize a map without ever taking a step. That is being religious without being spiritual. You can also walk a mountain without a map, finding your own way up. That is being spiritual without being religious.

If you look at major traditions—Christianity, Judaism, Islam, Hinduism, Buddhism—they appear different on the surface. Different holidays, different names for the Divine, whether that is God, Source, the Universe, or Creator. But they share common ground. Each teaches that your true self exists within you, whether called the Kingdom of God, Fitra, or Buddha Nature. Each warns that chasing status and approval leads to suffering, whether named Sin, Ego, or Attachment. Each points toward peace as the ultimate goal—Shalom, Shanti, or "the peace that surpasses understanding."

Christianity is my primary tradition, but I draw wisdom from many sources. From Buddhism, I learned that everything is connected—humans, animals, plants, the sun. This awareness makes me more conscientious of how my actions affect the collective, no matter how small the action seems.

I also appreciate traditions through their celebrations. When I learned that Dia de los Muertos includes a day for honoring pets who have passed, I didn't dismiss it as "not my religion." I thought it was beautiful, and now I take time to honor my fur babies on that day. I love that Diwali celebrates the triumph of good over evil and the power of togetherness. I can appreciate these truths without changing my own faith.

This is why I don't get upset about holiday greetings. If someone wishes me "Happy Hanukkah," I smile. I hope that when I say "Merry Christmas," they receive it the same way. It isn't about the religion. It is about one human being wishing another well.

And what if you don't believe in God or any higher power at all? You can still be spiritual. You can believe in the power of nature, in the value of a peaceful mind, or simply in love. Spirituality doesn't require a deity—it requires connection to something beyond yourself.

Your spiritual path should serve your Authentic Self, not constrain it. You can stand firmly in your own tradition while appreciating the view from someone else's mountain.

Intention of the Day
I will honor my spiritual path while staying open to wisdom from other sources.

Section 3: Your Truth

Distinguish your authentic voice from external programming

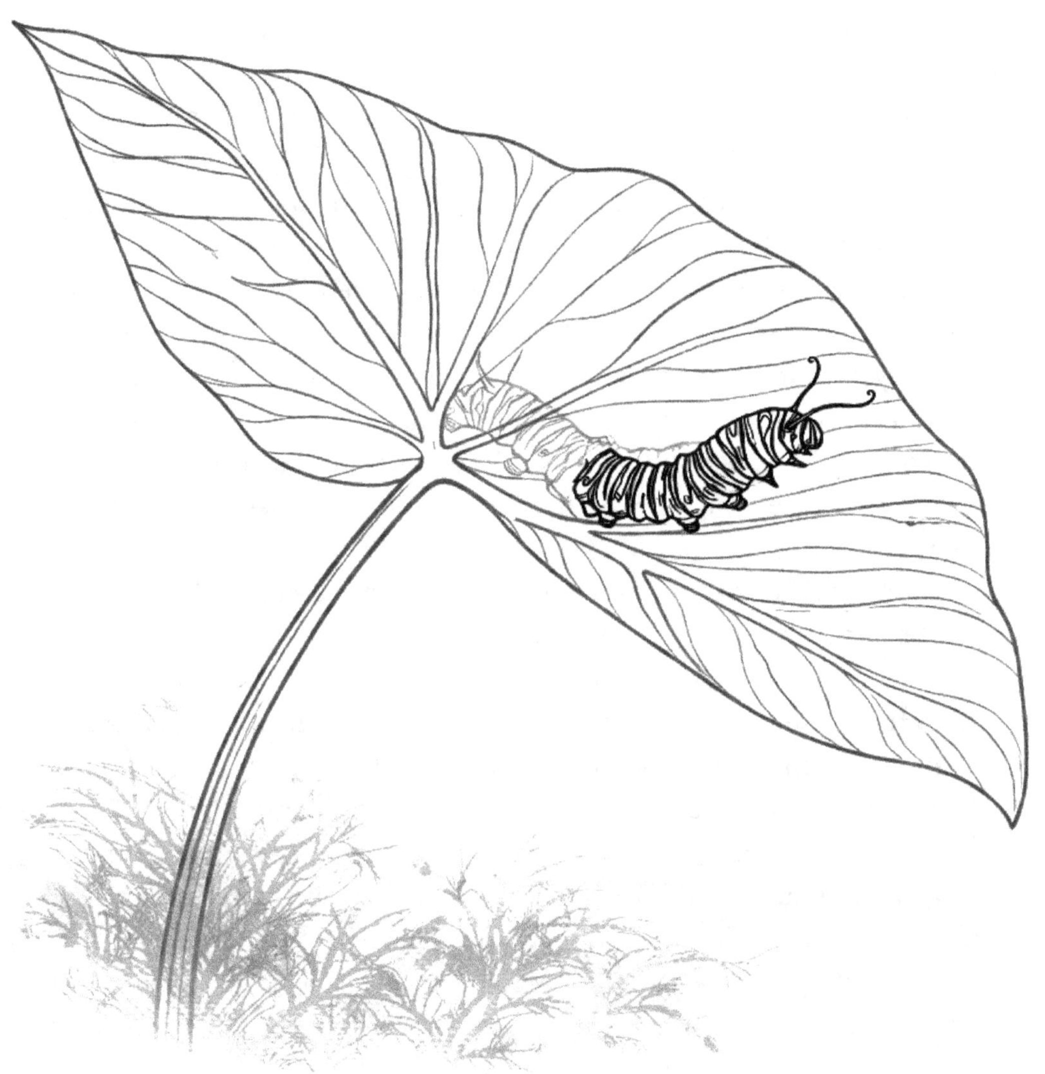

Feelings vs. Emotions: Know the Difference

Most people use "feelings" and "emotions" as if they mean the same thing. Understanding the difference can change how you understand yourself and build emotional intelligence that honors your Authentic Self.

Feelings are your internal reactions to an experience—what you become aware of inside when something happens. You might feel loss, betrayal, caught off guard, or sometimes something you can't name. Feelings are neutral. Emotions are how you mentally and physically respond to those feelings—thinking certain thoughts, crying, getting angry, staying calm, or feeling relieved. The same feeling can lead to different emotions depending on context. For example, when someone dies, you might feel loss. That feeling could express itself as sadness because you didn't want them to leave, relief because they're no longer suffering, or both at the same time. When someone jumps out to surprise you, you feel caught off guard. Your emotion could be surprise, anger, fear, or joy—depending on who did it, where it happened, and whether you like surprises.

Here's what makes this powerful: you can learn emotional responses that don't match your Authentic Self. When I started graduate school, experiments often failed. I would feel the failure but respond with calm, simply troubleshooting what went wrong. Then colleagues and professors told me my calm meant I didn't care. Worried about how others saw me, I learned to get angry, sad, and upset whenever experiments failed. These emotions became my default response to any failure. They drained my energy and created a negative environment around me. Years later, I recognized this wasn't healthy. I had to learn how to return to calm in the midst of failure while still communicating my feelings effectively. My original calm response was my Authentic Self. The anger and upset were my Created Self trying to meet others' expectations.

Understanding the difference between feelings and emotions helps you recognize which responses are truly yours and which you learned to perform. That's emotional intelligence, and it's essential for living authentically.

Later, in "Feel Everything Fully," you'll explore why expressing your emotions—rather than burying them—matters for both your mental and physical health.

Intention of the Day
I will notice my feelings and choose emotional responses that honor my Authentic Self.

You Are Fine as You Are

Are there things you wish you were brave enough to say or do? Do you wish you looked or thought differently than you do? That voice urging you to be someone else—that's your Created Self, echoing expectations you absorbed from family, culture, and society. But your Authentic Self knows something different: you are fine as you are.

Consider that the things you see as shortcomings might actually help others in ways you can't predict. I keep my hair very short—almost bald. Some people disapprove. They believe women should have long hair, that short natural hair isn't feminine enough or signals rebellion. But Black women approach me regularly in public, asking what motivated me to cut mine. Some want to reclaim the time and money they spend on salon visits. Others are dealing with hair thinning from menopause or alopecia. After we talk, they often say they feel empowered to make the same choice. What some see as my shortcoming, others see as permission to embrace their own shortcomings.

Your perceived flaws might be exactly what someone else needs to see. Beating yourself up does no good to your spirit. It weighs you down and subtracts from the good energy you could be putting into the world. As RuPaul says, "If you can't love yourself, how in the hell are you gonna love somebody else?"

Let go of the shoulda-coulda-wouldas. Let your self-love grow.

Intention of the Day
I will notice one self-criticism and release it so that self-love can grow.

Value Yourself

We make promises to ourselves every day: to exercise, eat better, rest more, finish that project. But how often do you actually keep them?

Think about it. You'd never cancel on a friend three times in a row without feeling terrible about it. You'd never repeatedly break promises to someone you love and expect the relationship to stay healthy. Yet we cancel on ourselves constantly—and barely notice.

This happens because your Created Self learned to prioritize everyone else's needs above your own. You go out of your way to help others with their problems, then feel too tired and overwhelmed to address your own. Things fall into disarray. Taking care of yourself gets even harder. The cycle continues.

I lived this pattern for years. I would exhaust myself helping others while my own life floundered. Eventually, I made a decision: my problems get addressed before I extend myself to help with someone else's. My business tasks come before helping others with theirs. I set boundaries now so the time I used to give away goes back to me first.

This isn't selfish. It's self-respect. If you made the same promises to someone you loved and didn't follow through, how would they feel? Dismissed. Unimportant. Not worth the effort. When you break promises to yourself, you send that same message to your own soul.

Your Authentic Self knows you deserve the same consideration you give others. Today, make one promise to yourself—and keep it.

Intention of the Day
I will keep one promise to myself today so I remember my worth.

Celebrate

Your Created Self measures accomplishments by others' expectations. Did they approve? Were they impressed? Did you make them proud? When your happiness depends on others' approval, you're set up to fail. You can't please everyone. And not everyone will get what you overcame.

Imagine choosing your own measuring stick for success. Imagine how much more meaningful your accomplishments would be if the driving force were purely internal. Your joy and pride would be bigger, stronger, and longer-lasting, because you wouldn't be giving that energy away to family, friends, bosses, or anyone else expecting you to make them proud. It would be yours alone.

Remember when I squatted to grab something from under the sink after eight years of not being able to? When I shared this with others, most responded with a bland "oh, that's nice." They'd never experienced similar limitations. They didn't realize what a big deal it was. But I didn't need them to. I basked in the achievement regardless.

Whether it's making a quilt, finishing a degree, losing weight, or simply getting out of bed to face the day, acknowledge every accomplishment that is meaningful to you. You get to decide what counts. Your Authentic Self knows what you overcame to get here—even if no one else does.

Each celebration is fuel for a happy you.

Intention of the Day
I will celebrate one accomplishment today, even if no one else does.

Your Birthday is a National Holiday

Your Created Self may have taught you that birthdays are for children. That making a fuss over yourself is selfish or immature. That once you're grown, the day should pass like any other.

But think about what a national holiday honors. A holiday marks something important—an event, a person, or a value that shaped the world. It gives people permission to step back from everyday duties. It makes room for celebration, reflection, and rest.

Your birthday deserves the same kind of respect.

Think about what your existence has made possible. The smiles and laughter you've brought to others. The moments when someone felt loved because you were there. The times you helped simply by being you—because of your presence, your skills, or your timing. The relationships you've supported or created. The things you've improved just by showing up.

These things matter. They ripple outward in ways you may never fully see.

So treat your birthday like the holiday it is. Take a break from the "shoulds" and the busy work. Celebrate with people who truly honor you—or celebrate quietly in your own way. Reflect on the good your life has brought into the world. And rest, because you deserve a day that belongs to you.

And if birthdays are painful for you, that's okay too. You can honor the day in a gentle way—through rest, prayer, journaling, nature, or a quiet treat. You still matter.

Your Authentic Self does not need permission to mark your own arrival. The day you were born changed things. That is worth celebrating—not because of what you've achieved, but because you exist.

Intention of the Day
I will honor my next birthday as a holiday, so I remember that my existence matters.

Do It Again

Are you afraid to live the life you dream of? Does it feel daunting to try something new that calls to your soul? Are you fearful of people judging the authentic you? Do you worry about failing to reach new heights if you try?

There is no need.

Your Created Self thrives on fear. It replays past failures, imagines future rejection, and whispers that this time will be different—that you'll fall short. It wants you to stay small because small feels safe.

But your Authentic Self knows the truth. It remembers what you've already done.

Trust that because you've had ideas, breakthroughs, dreams, and visions become reality, it will happen again.

Trust that because you overcame challenges before, you will do it again.

Trust that because you've had family, friends, coworkers, mentors, neighbors, and strangers support your goals in the past, they will do it again.

Trust that because you've previously found tools, resources, and opportunities to bring your visions into reality, you will find them again.

This isn't wishful thinking. It's evidence. Your life is full of proof that you can face hard things and come through. Every obstacle you've navigated, every fear you've pushed past, every dream you've brought to life—these aren't accidents. They're patterns. They reveal who you are when you trust yourself enough to try.

Your Authentic Self holds this history. It doesn't forget what you're capable of, even when fear tries to convince you otherwise. When doubt creeps in, let your Authentic Self remind you: you've done hard things before. You've surprised yourself before. You've succeeded before.

You've done it before. So there's nothing to fear. Do it again.

Intention of the Day
I will remember my past successes today so that I trust myself to try again.

You are Significant

If you've been ignored, dismissed, berated, taken advantage of, belittled, or underestimated, you may have felt like a waste of space—unloved, invisible, or like a doormat. These experiences can convince you that something is fundamentally wrong with you. But that feeling doesn't reflect the truth. It reflects what others projected onto you.

Consider what would remain if you removed your Created Self—the part shaped by parents, relatives, coworkers, media, and culture. What would be left?

You would be left with your Authentic Self. The part of you that is kind, brave, loving, loyal, and open-minded. The part that was brought into this world as beautifully as the trees, mountains, butterflies, and dolphins. The natural, untouched you is pure and worthy. You know this is true, even when the world makes you forget.

The people who made you feel insignificant were not responding to who you actually are. They were responding to their own pain, insecurity, or limitations. When someone belittles you, they often do so to quiet the doubts they carry about themselves. Their behavior reveals their struggle, not your worth.

This is why forgiveness becomes possible. You are not forgiving them because what they did was acceptable. You are forgiving them because holding onto resentment keeps their voice alive in your head. Forgiveness releases their power over how you see yourself. It allows you to return to the truth: you are significant simply because you exist.

Your Authentic Self has always known this. The doubt was never yours—it was handed to you. You can hand it back.

Intention of the Day
I will release one person's power over how I see myself so I can return to my truth.

You are a Survivor

Whether it was not passing an exam or placing last in a marathon, you made it through. Whether it was a very long day at work or moving into a new home, you've done it before and can do it again. Whether it was an abusive relationship or grieving the loss of a loved one, you're still here.

Surviving doesn't mean the pain is gone. It doesn't mean you're fully healed or that everything feels okay. It means you kept going when part of you wanted to stop. That persistence—even when it felt like barely hanging on—is proof of something powerful within you.

The fact that you're still here, drawing breath within this human experience, reveals strength, courage, resilience, and resourcefulness. These qualities don't belong to your Created Self, the part shaped by external expectations. They belong to your Authentic Self—the part of you that refuses to be extinguished no matter what life throws at you.

After leaving graduate school, I didn't have a job lined up. I found one two months later. Since then, I've left two other jobs that felt unbearable—each time without a new position secured. I always gave the company-required notice so I would remain eligible for rehire in case circumstances there improved. Friends worried and questioned whether leaving was the right decision. I told them that after spending eight and a half years in graduate school out of fear, I would never let any job hold me hostage again. As long as I had enough savings to leave properly, I trusted myself to land on my feet. And each time, I did.

That trust came from remembering what I'd already survived. You have that same evidence in your own life. Every struggle you've faced and moved through is proof that you can face the next one too.

Life itself is the prize. You're still in the race.

Intention of the Day
I will remember one thing I survived so I can trust myself to face what comes next.

Speaking Your Truth

You know what you really think. The question is whether you let yourself say it.

Maybe you soften your opinions so others won't push back. Maybe you agree with things you don't actually believe to keep the peace. Maybe you swallow your needs because asking feels selfish or dangerous. Each time you silence yourself, you move a little further from your Authentic Self.

This is your Created Self at work. From childhood, you learned that certain truths were unwelcome. Disagreement led to conflict. Expressing needs led to disappointment or rejection. Having your own opinions led to being labeled difficult. So you adapted. You became skilled at reading rooms, anticipating reactions, and editing yourself before you even spoke. This kept you connected—but at a cost.

The cost is exhaustion. It takes enormous energy to constantly filter yourself. It takes even more energy to keep track of which version of you showed up where. And underneath all that management lives a quiet grief: the grief of not being known, because you haven't let yourself be seen.

Here's what your Authentic Self knows: speaking your truth is not the same as speaking harshly.

Honesty doesn't require cruelty. You can express a different opinion without attacking someone else's. You can ask for what you need without demanding or manipulating. You can say no without offering a dissertation of justifications. You can share how something affected you without blaming or shaming the other person.

The difference is intention. Are you speaking to be heard or to wound? Are you expressing your truth or punishing someone for not already knowing it? Your Authentic Self speaks to connect, clarify, and honor what's real. It doesn't use honesty as a weapon.

Fear of rejection keeps many of us silent. We imagine the worst—that people will leave, judge, or attack if we say what we really think. Sometimes that fear is based on past experience. People did leave. They did judge. But staying silent to avoid rejection means rejecting yourself first. And the relationships you maintain through self-abandonment aren't relationships with the real you. They're relationships with your performance.

You deserve to be known. That requires letting yourself be heard.

Start small. Notice one moment today when you're tempted to filter yourself. Ask: What would I say if I trusted that my voice mattered? You don't have to say it out loud—not yet. Just notice what your truth actually is. That awareness is the first step toward expression.

Speaking your truth gets easier with practice. Each time you let your real voice emerge—and discover that you survive the response—your confidence builds. Some people will welcome your authenticity. Others may not. Both responses give you valuable information about who belongs in your life.

Your Authentic Self has been waiting to speak. Give it permission.

Intention of the Day
I will notice one truth I'm tempted to silence so that I remember my voice matters.

Living Your Truth Daily

Living as your Authentic Self means honoring every part of who you are—your thoughts, feelings, and emotions. These allow your soul to express itself fully. But you might bury your true nature to please others. You hide your happiness so others don't feel jealous. You mask your sadness to avoid seeming ungrateful. You cover up grief or anger to keep others comfortable. When you do these things, you bury who you truly are.

Imagine two friends receive promotions at work. One celebrates openly, sharing her excitement with family and friends. The other downplays her achievement, telling people it's "not a big deal" because she worries they'll think she's bragging. The first friend honors her authentic joy. The second suppresses hers to manage others' potential reactions. Both got the same promotion, but only one gets to fully experience the happiness that comes with it.

Suppressing your thoughts and emotions takes much more effort than you realize. This drains your energy and often leads to physical or mental illness. Your mind and body work together to maintain health. When your mind won't process heavy feelings, your body takes on that load. If this continues too long, your body burns out. This can show up as diabetes, high blood pressure, arthritis, and other chronic diseases.

You must process every emotion, not just positive ones. Surprise, disgust, loneliness, calm, courage—all deserve to be felt and understood. This honors your identity while protecting your well-being. Don't stuff away your feelings. Hiding your emotions is hiding your identity. Express yourself freely with grace and strength. If you struggle alone, ask for help. A coach, therapist, mentor, or friend will understand you. Support is available for your journey toward living authentically. You deserve to be you.

Intention of the Day
I will honor and express my Authentic Self with grace today.

Signs You're Performing

In "Speaking Your Truth," you explored what it means to let your authentic voice emerge. But what about the moments when you don't? How do you recognize when you've slipped into performance mode—when your Created Self has taken over without you noticing?

The good news is that noticing is itself a form of self-awareness. You can't return to your Authentic Self until you recognize you've drifted. Learning the signs is how you find your way back.

YOUR BODY KNOWS FIRST

Your body often signals inauthenticity before your mind catches up. Pay attention to tension—especially in your neck, shoulders, jaw, or stomach. Notice if your breathing becomes shallow or your smile feels forced. After certain interactions, do you feel drained rather than energized? That exhaustion is data.

My neck and shoulders tense whenever I'm not being authentic. I've also noticed my body reacts when others are performing—like colleagues who would say one thing in team discussions when the manager wasn't around, then say the opposite when she appeared. That inconsistency frustrated me deeply. If we had banded together and spoken our truth, we could have created positive change. But performance was safer than authenticity, so nothing shifted.

Sometimes we perform because we're in environments where everyone else is. Recognizing that pattern helps you decide whether to break it—or whether you're in a space that will never reward your authenticity.

YOUR MIND GETS LOUD

When you're performing, your inner dialogue intensifies. You rehearse what to say before you say it. You monitor others' reactions mid-conversation, adjusting in real time. You second-guess yourself constantly—*Was that okay? Did I say too much? Do they think I'm strange?* Your inner critic grows louder, evaluating every word.

This mental noise is exhausting because you're running two tracks simultaneously: the conversation happening out loud and the surveillance happening inside your head.

YOUR BEHAVIOR SHIFTS

Notice if you over-explain, trying to make yourself acceptable. Notice if you apologize for things that don't require apology. Do you agree with opinions you don't actually share? Laugh at jokes that aren't funny to you? Say "I don't mind" when you do mind? These small betrayals of your truth accumulate.

YOUR EMOTIONS SEND SIGNALS

Resentment often builds when you've been performing too long. You've given so much of yourself away that anger starts seeping through. You might also feel invisible—despite being present, you sense that no one actually knows you. That loneliness comes from hiding in plain sight.

RETURNING TO YOURSELF

Once you notice you're performing, you can return. Try this: pause and take one slow breath. Place your attention in your body. Then ask yourself quietly: *What's true for me right now?* You don't have to say it aloud. Simply reconnecting with your truth interrupts the performance.

Everyone slips into Created Self mode sometimes. This isn't failure— it's being human in a world that often rewards performance over authenticity. What matters is building the awareness to notice and the gentleness to return without self-judgment.

Your Authentic Self is never gone. It's simply waiting for you to remember it's there.

Intention of the Day
I will notice one sign that I'm performing so that I can gently return to myself.

Section 4: Your Trauma

Process and release what's held you back

Accepting Hurt

When someone hurts you, the pain is real. The anger is real. The resentment is real. You are entitled to feel every bit of what you feel—and depending on the depth of the wound, resentment may seem like the only option available. Please know: there is nothing wrong with you for struggling to let go.

But there is another path. Even painful experiences can teach us something. Somewhere within the hurt lies a lesson—about your boundaries, your needs, your values, or how you want to be treated. Finding that lesson doesn't erase the pain. It gives the pain a purpose.

Here is what matters: moving from hurt to growth is a process, not a switch. You don't flip from resentment to gratitude overnight. You move through stages, and resentment is often the first one. That's not failure. That's being human.

Your Created Self may want to stay in resentment because it feels protective. Holding onto anger can seem safer than vulnerability. But your Authentic Self knows that resentment kept too long becomes a weight you carry everywhere. It occupies mental and emotional space that could hold peace instead.

The goal isn't to rush yourself toward acceptance. The goal is to remain open to eventually seeing the lesson when you're ready. Some hurts take weeks to process. Others take years. There is no timeline you're supposed to follow. What matters is not closing the door permanently on the possibility of healing.

I was sixteen, walking through my high school courtyard, still grieving my grandfather's murder. I asked myself, "Why does evil exist?" A voice in my head replied: "So that you know what good looks like."

That voice—my Authentic Self speaking—gave meaning to unbearable pain. The lesson didn't erase what happened. But it gave the hurt purpose. Maybe betrayal by a friend taught you what loyalty truly looks like. Maybe a painful breakup revealed patterns you needed to change. Maybe losing a job showed you what kind of work actually sustains you. The lesson emerges when you're ready to see it, not before.

Be patient with yourself. Healing isn't a straight line, and there's no timeline you're supposed to follow. You're allowed to acknowledge the resentment without living in it forever. Trust that your Authentic Self will guide you toward the lesson when you're ready—not when someone else thinks you should be. The healing is in the process, not just the destination.

Intention of the Day
I will be patient with my healing and stay open to finding the lesson within the hurt.

Feel Everything Fully

For years, when I held in extreme anger, my entire abdomen would be so sore the next day I could barely walk. I didn't feel safe talking to others about my anger, so I kept it buried. My body paid the price. When trauma teaches you that certain emotions aren't safe to express—whether anger, grief, or even joy—your Created Self learns to suppress your truth. But that suppression doesn't make the emotions disappear.

Thoughts, feelings, and emotions are how your Authentic Self expresses itself in this world. When you bury them to meet others' expectations, you're not just managing stress—you're betraying who you are.

From childhood, we learn to hide certain emotions. Don't express happiness so others don't get jealous. Don't show sadness so you don't seem ungrateful. Don't reveal grief so you don't worsen someone else's pain. Don't display anger so others don't feel unsafe. Your Created Self learned to suppress your truth to keep peace and meet expectations.

But suppressing emotions doesn't make them disappear. It forces your body to carry what your mind refuses to process. The mind and body work together to maintain your health. When one struggles, the other compensates. If your mind won't process emotions, your body absorbs the burden. Over time, this leads to diabetes, high blood pressure, arthritis, and other chronic conditions. Many diseases would be less common if we fully felt and processed our emotions.

After I left graduate school and started building my tribe, I found people I felt safe with. I began talking through my anger instead of burying it. The abdominal pain stopped completely. That's what happens when you honor your Authentic Self by feeling fully.

Every emotion deserves to be felt and understood—surprise, disgust, loneliness, calm, courage, all of them. Feeling your emotions isn't weakness. It's honoring your truth and protecting your health.

If you struggle to express yourself, ask for help. A trusted friend who simply listens, a therapist who holds safe space, or even a private journal — start where you can. Expression doesn't require an audience. It requires honesty. You deserve to feel. You deserve to be you. Begin there, and the rest will follow.

Intention of the Day
I will feel my emotions fully today instead of burying them.

Recognizing Trauma Responses

Before you can heal from past wounds, you have to recognize how they're still showing up in your life.

Many behaviors that feel like "just who I am" are actually survival strategies your Created Self developed long ago. People-pleasing kept you safe from rejection. Hypervigilance helped you anticipate danger. Avoidance protected you from pain. Perfectionism made you feel worthy of love. These responses made sense when you needed them. The question is whether they still serve you now.

People-pleasing means saying yes when you mean no, abandoning your needs to keep others comfortable. Hypervigilance is constantly scanning for danger, unable to relax even when safe. Avoidance steers you away from anything that might trigger difficult emotions. Perfectionism convinces you that you must be flawless to be worthy of love.

I discovered this through a friend whose life circumstances mirrored mine. We faced similar disappointments, disrespect, and boundary crossings. But while I responded with anger, she remained calm. When I asked how, she explained her perspective: human beings are flawed, so mistakes are expected. When they don't happen, that's the surprise worth celebrating. Her words showed me that my anger wasn't inevitable—it was a pattern I could examine and change.

That recognition was the first step.

Trauma responses show up in many forms. Some people become controlling, trying to manage every outcome so nothing catches them off guard. Others become judgmental, creating distance before anyone can hurt them. Some fall into victim mentality, believing they have no power to change their circumstances. None of these responses make you broken. They reveal where healing wants to happen.

Notice your patterns without judgment. When do you people-please instead of speaking your truth? When does hypervigilance exhaust you? Where does avoidance keep you stuck? Your Authentic Self isn't asking you to fix everything today. It's inviting you to see clearly—because awareness is where healing begins.

Intention of the Day
I will notice one pattern in myself with curiosity so that healing can begin.

Your Body Remembers

You've already learned that your mind and body communicate constantly. When it comes to trauma, this connection goes even deeper: your body stores what your mind can't fully process.

Think back to what you read in the introduction. During my years in graduate school, my body was screaming that something was wrong. Tension headaches. Muscle spasms. IBS and gastritis. Rashes and random vomiting. Hair loss. I kept pushing through, telling myself these symptoms were just stress. But my body was holding what my mind refused to acknowledge—that I was living a life that was slowly destroying me.

Your body might be doing the same thing. Chronic pain that doctors can't explain. Tightness in your chest or throat. A stomach that knots up in certain situations. Fatigue that sleep doesn't fix. These aren't signs that something is wrong with you. They're signals that your body is carrying something that needs release.

The good news is that what the body stores, the body can also let go. For me, healing my IBS required more than changing my circumstances. It took a combination of breathwork meditation, massage, hot baths, and regular exercise. These practices gave my body permission to release what it had been holding for years.

Remember the modalities you explored in Section 1—Reiki, acupuncture, stretching, grounding techniques. These aren't just for daily maintenance. They can help your body process old wounds. Body-based therapies work because they speak your body's language, accessing what talk alone sometimes can't reach.

Some of these practices require professional support—and investment. If cost is a barrier, focus on what's freely available: breathwork costs nothing. Hot baths use resources you already have. Walking and stretching require only your body and a few minutes of time. Start where you can. Your body will meet you there.

Your Authentic Self lives in your body, not just your mind. When you listen to your body's messages and offer it care, you create space for deep healing.

Intention of the Day
I will listen to one message my body is sending so that healing can reach deeper.

Honoring Conflicting Emotions in Grief

Now that you understand how trauma shows up in your body, let's look at one of the most universal forms of trauma: loss. Whether you're grieving a person, a relationship, or a version of yourself, these next three articles will help you honor what grief asks of you.

"HERE" BY KELLY NEMBHARD

When I lose, I isolate.
When I lose, I'm sad.
When I lose, I hurt.
But, when I lose, I'm glad?

I say, "they're in a better place."
I know that this is true.
But, if I say I want them back,
Then, doesn't that make me cruel?

I know that they're not "gone".
I know that they're still "here".
They're here now more than before,
Because I "feel" them everywhere.

I miss the feel, the smell, the voice...
I miss seeing them here.
And now that they are "here" instead,
I'll use my other eyes, skin, nose, and ears.

***

The night my father died, I heard his voice before bed. He appeared in my dreams. The following week, while visiting my aunt in a Baltimore hospital, she asked how things went back home in Jamaica. A male orderly walked in at that exact moment. His name tag read "Victor O."—my father's name was Victor Oliver Nembhard. These signs told me he was still present, just differently.

Later, I wrote this poem trying to make sense of what I was experiencing. My father had been on life support before he died. I wondered what his life would have looked like if he had survived—would he have fully recovered, or would complications have reduced the quality of his remaining life? People said he was in a better place, and I agreed. But that truth did not erase how much I missed him.

Grief asks us to hold conflicting emotions. You can know someone is in a better place and still ache for them. You can feel relief that their suffering ended while mourning everything you lost. You can sense their spirit everywhere and miss their physical presence desperately. None of these truths cancel out the others.

This isn't a sign that something is wrong with you or that you're grieving incorrectly. The presence of opposing feelings is proof that your love was real and multi-dimensional. Simple losses would bring simple grief. Complex love brings complex grief.

Your Authentic Self knows grief is not either/or—it is both/and. You can believe someone is free from suffering and still wish they were here. You can feel grateful for the end of pain and devastated by absence. Your Created Self might judge these feelings as wrong or selfish. But your Authentic Self understands that conflict is where honest grief lives.

When we honor our authentic grief, we stop asking if our emotions are "right" and start noticing what is actually true. This is how we process loss—not by following someone else's timeline or emotional script, but by trusting our own experience.

Your grief is yours alone. Feel the conflicting emotions. Notice how presence shifts from physical to energetic. When someone tells you how you should feel or how long grief should last, remember: they're speaking from their Created Self's need for order and timeline. Your Authentic Self knows grief has its own rhythm, and that's the only timeline that matters. Trust that your Authentic Self knows how to grieve, even when it looks different from what you expected.

Intention of the Day
I will allow myself to feel conflicting emotions about my loss today.

Your Grief Matters

When someone you care about dies, you might hear: "But you barely knew them" or "I don't understand why you're so upset." These responses can make you feel alone in your grief, like maybe your pain isn't valid.

Here's what I want you to know: your grief matters.

Every soul is unique and affects others in ways we can't fully see. A hug you gave might have kept someone from deep depression. Your achievements might have inspired someone to keep trying. Sharing your story might have helped someone feel less alone. Even giving a child a piece of candy might have been the first moment they realized they truly matter. Simple acts can have huge impacts.

That's why your grief is valid, even when others don't understand it.

I once grieved a high school bully who tormented me for five years. She said horrible things to me constantly. Then one Friday, she was civil—gentle, sweet, with a slight smile. Two days later, she drowned at a beach. I cried at her funeral. I grieved the sweetness I'd witnessed, the lost chance to reconcile, and the horrific way she died. Her best friend's profound pain broke my heart. People didn't understand my tears. But my grief was real.

I've also grieved Chadwick Boseman and Robin Williams, even though I never met them. When I was four or five, I grieved how Jesus was killed. Grief doesn't require a perfect relationship or any relationship at all. It honors the impact a soul had on your life, whether through direct connection, inspiration, or simply their humanity.

I've grieved my grandmother's grandmother, whom I never met. She was thirteen, playing in a field in Ghana with two friends her age, when white men jumped out of the bushes with nets. They chased the children, caught them in the nets, and took them straight to a ship. My grandmother told me her strongest memory was her great-grandmother crying on her deathbed to be able to go back to Ghana, that she wanted to go home. She died surrounded by children and grandchildren—but she never saw her homeland again. I grieve for her unfulfilled dream, for the home she was stolen from, for the childhood that ended in those nets.

Grief doesn't require death at all. You can grieve dreams that didn't come true, futures that will never happen, and hopes that quietly died while you were still living.

The rejection letter from your dream college. The relationship that ended before it became the marriage you'd imagined. The career path that closed when your health changed. The child you hoped to have but couldn't. The version of your country or community you believed was possible but hasn't materialized. These losses are real. They deserve to be mourned.

Your Created Self may insist you have no right to grieve what you never had. It whispers that you're being dramatic, that others have "real" problems, that you should just move on. But your Authentic Self knows: you're not grieving something imaginary. You're grieving a future you genuinely believed in—one you could see, feel, and almost touch. The loss of that future leaves a hole, even if no one else can see it.

If others don't understand your grief, that doesn't make it wrong. That person touched YOUR life specifically. Your grief reflects how meaningful their existence was to you.

If you find yourself minimizing your grief because "others had it worse" or "I shouldn't feel this way," stop. Pain isn't a competition. Your grief doesn't need to justify itself to anyone—including you.

Whether you're grieving a parent, child, friend, pet, leader, celebrity, or stranger, your grief matters. The depth of your pain is not up for debate or comparison. It's yours, and it's real.

Intention of the Day
I will honor my grief as valid, regardless of what others think.

Being Present While Grieving

When someone you love dies, staying in the present moment becomes almost impossible. The present means they're gone, and that pain feels too big to hold. Your mind does what minds do when overwhelmed—it tries to escape.

Finding out about their death is like a bomb going off inside you. The impact is so sharp and powerful that it damages your ability to stay present. The pain explodes outward, and suddenly you're thrown between past and future, unable to stand still in the now.

Your mind runs to the past—memories, regrets, the last time you saw them. You cling to those moments as if losing them risks losing the memories too. But dwelling there becomes painful, so your mind runs to the future. What will life be like without them? How will you manage? That feels overwhelming, so your mind runs back to the past. Back and forth, trying to escape the unbearable present.

When my father died, I found myself caught in this exact pattern. Thinking about all our memories together, then worrying about the aftermath—funeral planning, expenses, how others would behave, how my life was permanently changed. My mind couldn't settle.

This swinging back and forth IS grief. The frequency and intensity of switching between past and future is how grief shows up. How long it lasts depends on how long it takes to repair the damage to your ability to be present.

There's no quick fix, but understanding what's happening helps. When you notice your mind running, be gentle with yourself. Take three slow breaths. Feel your feet on the floor or your hands on your chest.

You're not doing grief wrong—this is grief itself. Let your mind wander when it needs to. This is how it copes.

Or name five things you can see right now—five concrete objects in your immediate surroundings. This simple act interrupts the swing and returns you to where you actually are: here, breathing, alive.

Be aware of when you need extra care and comfort, and seek it out. Your loved one would want that for you.

Intention of the Day
I will be gentle with my grieving mind so that healing can happen at its own pace.

Let Go of Anger

Grief isn't the only emotion that can trap you in the past. Anger and self-blame are equally powerful—and equally worth releasing. These next three articles guide you through that process.

Anger makes sense. When you've been dismissed, disrespected, or made to feel powerless, anger rises to protect you. It says: this matters. I matter. What happened wasn't okay. That response is valid—your anger is telling you something important. The question isn't whether your anger is justified. It's whether holding onto it continues to serve you.

I learned this at a hair salon. I'd gone to get my small Afro shaped. After my hair dried, the stylist started brushing it, and white flakes began falling everywhere. I asked if my scalp was that dry. She stopped, looked at the brush, and said, "I don't even think that's yours." The entire salon went dead quiet. Everyone waited to see how I'd react.

In that moment, I had a choice. I could yell at this stylist for putting a dirty brush in my hair. Or I could accept that whether I got angry or not,

I was never coming back. So I saved my energy. I simply chose to never return.

When you notice anger rising, pause. Take a deep breath. Then ask yourself: What about this situation is making me angry? What is my anger trying to protect? Does expressing this anger change anything, or does it just cost me energy? What action can I take instead that actually serves me?

Sometimes anger isn't about letting go—it's about speaking up. If someone violated your boundaries, your anger is information. It tells you a line was crossed. In these moments, anger serves you by demanding acknowledgment and change.

The question isn't "Should I be angry?" but "What does this anger want me to do?" Sometimes the answer is: walk away. Sometimes it's: have a difficult conversation. Sometimes it's: set a firmer boundary. Your Authentic Self knows the difference between anger that protects your well-being and anger that keeps you stuck in resentment.

These questions help you understand what anger is telling you without letting it take over. The goal isn't to suppress your feelings or pretend you're fine when you're not. It's to respond with intention rather than react from hurt. Sometimes the most powerful response to a situation isn't an outburst. It's a quiet decision to redirect your energy toward what actually matters.

If anger needs to move through you, give it safe outlet. Write an unsent letter saying everything you wish you could say. Move your body— walk fast, punch a pillow, dance hard. Talk it through with someone who won't try to fix it, just witness it. Anger isn't dangerous when it has room to exist. It's dangerous when it's trapped.

You don't have to let go of anger before you're ready. But when you are ready, your Authentic Self knows when to fight and when to walk away. Trust that knowing.

Intention of the Day
I will pause when anger rises and ask what it's protecting.

Let Go of Self-Blame

Self-blame wastes energy. It takes up brain space that could be used for bringing more positivity into your life. It doesn't fix anything—it only makes the situation worse.

Here's what makes self-blame especially damaging: you're with yourself twenty-four hours a day. When you blame someone else, they can be out of sight, out of mind. But when you blame yourself, there's no escape. Your Created Self—that inner critic shaped by years of internalized expectations—has unlimited access to remind you of every mistake, every should-have-known-better, every way you fell short.

I used to blame myself for not leaving graduate school sooner. I let fear hold me hostage for eight and a half years in an environment I hated. I spiraled into "what ifs"—how much further I'd be in my career, how much more money I'd have saved, whether I could have afforded a house by now. But I didn't know then what I know now—that everything would have worked out fine if I'd left sooner. There was no point in beating myself up about decisions made without the wisdom I've since gained.

You forgot to do something. Said the wrong thing. Made a mistake. How does self-blame make any of that better? It doesn't. So instead of punishing yourself, acknowledge what happened, make amends if needed, and move on. Ground yourself—breathe, take a walk, drink some tea—and redirect your energy toward what's next.

Taking responsibility isn't the same as self-blame. Responsibility says: "I made a mistake, and here's what I'll do differently." Self-blame says: "I'm a terrible person who always messes up." One creates growth. The other creates paralysis. Choose responsibility. Release blame.

From the Forgiveness meditation in the MyLife app: "It isn't easy being human. No one is perfect. Caught up in our emotions and distractions, it is easy to make mistakes. I forgive myself for any way that I have caused myself harm."

Your Authentic Self knows you deserve the same compassion you'd offer a friend. Give it to yourself.

Intention of the Day
I will replace self-blame with compassion so my energy serves me.

Pick Something to Forgive

Forgiveness is one of the hardest lessons in human life. But why? Many people struggle because they confuse forgiveness with condoning. They think forgiving means saying what happened was okay. It doesn't. Forgiveness means accepting that the wrong occurred and choosing to stop carrying it. You can forgive and still set boundaries. You can forgive and never let that person close again. Forgiveness isn't about letting them off the hook. It's about taking yourself off the hook—releasing the weight so you can move forward.

The Serenity Prayer offers a useful framework: "Grant me the serenity to accept the things I cannot change, the courage to change the things I can, and the wisdom to know the difference." You cannot change what happened. You can change how long you carry it. Accept the wrong and the lesson that came with it. Integrate that lesson into your life. Protect yourself from repeating the situation. After that, the need to keep replaying the hurt fades.

Here's what masters of forgiveness understand: it's a practice, not a one-time event. You don't wait for a special occasion. You build the habit by choosing something to release regularly—even small things. The driver who cut you off. The friend who forgot to call back. The coworker who took credit. Each act of forgiveness strengthens the muscle.

Start small. Forgive the driver who cut you off. Forgive yourself for sleeping through your alarm. Forgive the friend who forgot to call back. These small releases build capacity for bigger forgiveness when you're ready.

Forgiveness also means seeing people clearly. As the American rapper and songwriter DMX wisely said, "Always trust everyone to be themselves, but trust in the fact that you can see them well. It takes too much energy to not trust someone. Trust a snake to bite you, trust a liar to lie to you, trust a thief to steal from you." It also takes too much energy to wish people were different. Trust them to be who they've shown you they are, and protect yourself accordingly. You can forgive someone and still know exactly who you're dealing with.

When you forgive, you free up space in your mind. That space becomes peace.

Intention of the Day
I will forgive one thing today so I can reclaim my peace.

Boundaries as Healing

Arelative makes a cutting remark at a family gathering. You feel the sting, the familiar tightening in your chest. Words rise in your throat—but you swallow them. Someone catches your eye and gives you that look: Don't make a scene. Keep the peace.

So you do. Again.

Later, you replay the moment. You imagine what you could have said. You feel the anger settle into resentment; the resentment hardens into distance. And somewhere beneath all of it, a quiet question: Why do I keep allowing this?

You've done the inner work of releasing what no longer serves you—processing grief, anger, blame, and practicing forgiveness. Now it's time to protect yourself from future harm. That's where boundaries come in.

WHY BOUNDARIES FEEL SO HARD

If you struggle to set boundaries, you're not alone. And you're not broken. You're likely carrying patterns from a time when protecting yourself felt impossible.

Trauma teaches us that our needs don't matter. When you learned early that saying no led to punishment, withdrawal of love, or abandonment, your Created Self adapted. It built itself around keeping others comfortable, anticipating their reactions, and shrinking your needs to maintain connection. Boundaries feel threatening because your Created Self was designed to survive without them.

But here's what your Authentic Self knows: boundaries aren't selfish. They're an act of self-love.

Setting boundaries means honoring the truth that your needs matter as much as anyone else's. It means recognizing that relationships requiring you to abandon yourself aren't relationships—they're arrangements where you pay the cost. It means trusting that people who genuinely care about you will respect your limits, even if they're initially uncomfortable.

Understanding why boundaries feel difficult can help you move through the discomfort:

- **Fear of abandonment.** If love felt conditional growing up, setting boundaries can trigger terror that you'll be left. Your nervous system remembers what happened when you asserted yourself before.

- **Guilt from conditioning.** You may have absorbed the message that your needs are selfish, that good people put others first, that taking care of yourself means taking from someone else. This guilt isn't truth—it's programming.

- **Hypervigilance about reactions.** Trauma survivors often become experts at reading others' emotions. You might abandon a boundary the moment you sense displeasure because someone else's discomfort feels unbearable.

These responses made sense once. They helped you survive. But they're no longer serving your Authentic Self.

What Boundaries Look Like in Practice

I'm learning this lesson right now. I've been working on this book for over three years, and a big reason it's taken so long is that I kept prioritizing helping others with their needs. Recently, I found a hard copy of a draft article sitting in a pile of papers and felt irritated with myself. Why wasn't this done yet? The answer was clear: I hadn't protected my time and energy for what matters to me. So I started saying no more often—to requests, to favors, to the constant pull of other people's priorities. Each no has been an act of self-love that brings this book closer to your hands.

But the harder boundaries have been with people, not just time.

I grew up with relatives who had a habit of being disrespectful. I was encouraged to bite my tongue and keep the peace because they were blood. No matter how many times I felt disregarded or insulted, my loved ones told me that's just what family does.

After certain members of the family passed away, something shifted. I no longer felt obligated to keep the peace with people who I don't believe would donate a kidney if I needed it—or take a bullet for me. I don't even believe they love me. There was literally no incentive to keep them in my life.

Some family members still insist I should maintain communication with these relatives. "That's what family does. You might need them someday." I completely disagree. They're not my family. They're my relatives. And through them, I learned how I want to be treated—which is not the way they treat me.

So I have no communication with them. I wish them well, but I don't want them in my life.

I tell people all the time: if you add to the quality of my life, or have no effect on it whatsoever, we're good. Once you subtract from the quality of my life, you are no longer a person I will invest my time, energy, or resources in.

That clarity didn't come easily. It came from years of ignored boundaries finally demanding to be honored.

HOW TO BEGIN SETTING BOUNDARIES

Boundary-setting is a skill, and like any skill, it develops with practice. Here's how to start:

Recognize the need. Notice when resentment, exhaustion, or that familiar knot in your stomach appears. These feelings often signal that a boundary is needed. Your body knows before your mind does.

Give yourself permission. Before you say anything to anyone else, say this to yourself: I have the right to protect my time, energy, and peace. You don't need to earn this right. You already have it.

Communicate simply and clearly. Boundaries don't require lengthy explanations or justifications. The simpler, the better. Here are scripts you can use:

- "I can't take that on right now."
- "That doesn't work for me."
- "I need to think about that before I commit."
- "I'm not available for that conversation."
- "I wish you well, and I need distance."

Expect discomfort—yours and theirs. Guilt may flood you after setting a boundary. The other person may push back or express disappointment. This discomfort doesn't mean you did something wrong. It means you did something new.

Hold the line with compassion. You can be kind and still maintain your boundary. "I understand this is disappointing, but I'm not able to help this time." Compassion for others doesn't require abandoning yourself.

BOUNDARIES AND YOUR RELATIONSHIPS

Here's something important: boundaries don't destroy healthy relationships. They reveal which relationships were healthy to begin with.

People who respect you will adjust. They may need a moment, but they'll honor your limits. People who only valued what you could do for them will resist, guilt-trip, or withdraw. That reaction isn't evidence that you were wrong to set the boundary. It's evidence that the boundary was necessary.

As you practice, something shifts. The guilt becomes quieter. The fear loosens its grip. You start to trust that you can take care of yourself and maintain connection with people who genuinely love you. This is what healing looks like.

Your Authentic Self has been waiting for you to protect it. Every boundary you set is a message to yourself: I matter. My needs are valid. I am worth protecting.

That's not selfish. That's self-love.

Intention of the Day

I will set or hold one boundary today so that I honor my own needs.

Permission to Say No

You've learned that boundaries are essential for healing. You've explored how to recognize when you need them, give yourself permission to set them, and hold them with compassion. Now let's talk about the word that makes all of that possible—the word many trauma survivors struggle most to say.

Many say the most powerful word in any language is "love". But not enough appreciation has been given to its first runner-up: "no."

Pursuing your purpose requires protecting your time and energy. Every "yes" to something that doesn't align with your authentic goals is a "no" to what truly matters. When you understand this, "no" becomes more than boundary-setting—it becomes purpose-protection.

"No" packs quite a punch. It can break hearts, deplete self-esteem, and start conflict. But when used with grace and without fear, "no" is one of the most powerful tools in self-care. It shields you from people and commitments that will drain you dry. For trauma survivors who learned that saying "no" led to punishment, withdrawal of love, or danger, reclaiming this word is especially crucial—it's how you stop repeating patterns that once kept you safe but now keep you stuck.

Most of us, whether or not we've experienced trauma, struggle with the same pattern: we say "yes" too often because we're trying to be loved and appreciated. We make promises to prove our worth or avoid disappointing others. This is your Created Self at work—believing you must earn love through constant availability. But overcommitting sets you up for failure. You end up breaking promises, exhausting yourself, or resenting the very people you wanted to please.

Your Authentic Self knows the truth: you don't have to say "yes" to be worthy of love.

Before making any agreement, pause and ask yourself three questions. What will be the physical, mental, and emotional impact on me? Will saying "yes" put my existing commitments at risk? And honestly, what are the chances I'll follow through? If the answers reveal strain, conflict, or doubt, that's valuable information. Saying "no" protects both you and the person asking—they deserve a wholehearted "yes" or an honest "no," not a reluctant commitment you can't keep.

When I started living as my Authentic Self, saying "no" became easier. I stopped needing everyone's approval to feel worthy. The guilt faded. The freedom grew. You can experience this too.

Saying "no" isn't selfish. It's how you protect your energy for the commitments that truly matter—including the ones you've made to yourself.

Intention of the Day
I will say "no" when needed to protect my well-being and honor my commitments.

Making Space for Your Real Tribe

You've learned to say "no" to requests and obligations that drain you. But what about the people themselves? Sometimes the deepest act of self-care isn't saying "no" to what someone asks—it's saying "no" to the relationship entirely.

A woman once called me asking about Reiki for stress relief. When I asked what caused her stress, she said it was her family. They constantly criticized her choices. They judged her for never marrying. They disapproved of her not having children. They didn't like her career. Yet they relied on her for everything: pet sitting, babysitting, rides, money. I asked if she even liked these people. She said, "No."

"Then why do you spend time with them?"

"I worry about who'll take care of me when I'm older."

"Do you trust them to take care of you?"

"No."

I paused. "Then what are you getting from this relationship right now?"

She couldn't answer. What she could say was that without them, she'd have peace and time for herself.

Here's what I've learned. Toxic people take up space meant for your real tribe—those who truly care about you. When you keep relationships that drain you, you're telling the universe you're not ready for genuine connection. The people who will accept your Authentic Self, who will show up for you without conditions, are waiting. But there's no room for them while you're trying to earn love from people who've never freely offered it.

Cutting people out isn't easy. Fear of the unknown can feel worse than the pain you already know. You might wonder: "What if I need them? What if I'm wrong? What if I end up alone?" These worries are real. But staying requires seeing clearly what you're choosing.

Your Authentic Self knows the difference between relationships that feed you and relationships that drain you. Trust that knowing. When you're ready to let go, you make space for what truly sustains you.

This is how you move from surviving to thriving—not by keeping everyone, but by keeping the right ones. Your real tribe is waiting.

Intention of the Day
I will make room for healthy relationships by releasing the ones that drain me.

Self-Care Tip: Talk Therapy

Talk therapy involves meeting with someone to discuss your thoughts, feelings, and emotions for the purpose of seeking clarity and understanding in your life. It's a powerful form of self-care that helps you process experiences, work through challenges, and develop healthier patterns.

Licensed therapists, counselors, and psychotherapists provide talk therapy. They're trained to diagnose and treat mental health conditions like depression, anxiety, trauma, and OCD. They help you understand how past experiences shape current behaviors and guide you toward healing.

If you're experiencing persistent sadness, panic attacks, trauma flashbacks, suicidal thoughts, or other mental health challenges, seeking a licensed therapist is essential. These are medical concerns that require professional treatment.

Health coaches like myself offer a different kind of support. We help clients set goals, make behavior changes, and develop healthier habits. We don't diagnose or treat mental health conditions. Instead, we focus on what you want to change and support you in building habits that last. As a health coach, I often recommend clients work with a therapist alongside coaching for the best outcomes. Both can work together beautifully.

Taking the step to seek talk therapy is an act of self-care and courage. Whether you're working through specific challenges or simply want support in understanding yourself better, the right professional can make a meaningful difference in your well-being. The next article, "Self-Care Tip: When to Seek Professional Help," offers guidance on finding the right therapist for your needs.

Self-Care Tip: When to Seek Professional Help

This article covers more ground than most because the topic deserves careful attention. Throughout this section, you've explored tools for processing trauma, setting boundaries, and reclaiming your personal power. These practices are valuable—and sometimes they're not enough. Recognizing when you need professional support isn't weakness. It's wisdom. It's your Authentic Self saying: I deserve more help than I can give myself right now.

If you turned to this article before reading anything else in this section, that's okay. You're exactly where you need to be. Reading this is itself an act of self-care.

SIGNS THAT PROFESSIONAL HELP IS NEEDED

How do you know when self-care has reached its limits? Watch for these signals:

- **Symptoms interfering with daily life.** You're struggling to work, maintain relationships, sleep, eat, or complete basic tasks. What used to feel manageable now feels impossible.
- **Thoughts of self-harm or suicide.** If you're having thoughts of hurting yourself or ending your life, please reach out immediately. This is urgent, and support is available.
- **Patterns that self-care hasn't shifted.** You've tried meditation, journaling, boundaries, and grounding techniques. You've done the work. But the same patterns keep showing up, and you feel stuck.
- **Trauma flashbacks or intrusive memories.** The past keeps intruding on the present—through nightmares, sudden emotional flooding, or memories that hijack your day without warning.
- **Physical symptoms with no medical explanation.** Doctors can't find a cause for your chronic pain, fatigue, digestive issues, or other symptoms. Your body may be holding what your mind hasn't processed.

I experienced this during graduate school. I kept seeing my primary care physician for IBS symptoms. Once she determined the diagnosis, she referred me to Counseling and Psychological Services. She explained that IBS involves a dysregulation of the gut-brain connection, often linked to stress. My body had been telling me something my mind wasn't ready to hear. That referral was a turning point.

TYPES OF MENTAL HEALTH PROFESSIONALS

In "Self-Care Tip: Talk Therapy," you learned the difference between psychotherapy and coaching. Now let's look at the different types of mental health professionals so you can find the right match for what you're experiencing.

- **Therapist, Counselor, or Psychotherapist.** These professionals provide talk therapy to help you understand patterns, process emotions, and develop healthier ways of coping. They treat conditions like depression, anxiety, and trauma. This is often a good starting point if you're unsure what you need.
- **Psychiatrist.** A medical doctor who specializes in mental health. Psychiatrists can prescribe medication, which may help when symptoms have a biological component—such as severe depression, anxiety disorders, or PTSD that hasn't responded to therapy alone. Many people work with both a psychiatrist and a therapist.
- **Trauma-Informed Therapist.** A therapist with specialized training in how trauma affects the mind and body. They understand that certain approaches can retraumatize rather than heal, and they create safety throughout the process. If you know trauma is at the root of your struggles, seek someone with this specific training.
- **EMDR Practitioner.** EMDR stands for Eye Movement Desensitization and Reprocessing. This approach helps your brain process traumatic memories that feel stuck. It's particularly effective for PTSD, flashbacks, and intrusive memories. EMDR practitioners are trained and certified in this specific technique.

- **Somatic Therapist.** Remember what you learned in "Your Body Remembers"—the body stores what the mind can't process. Somatic therapists specialize in body-based approaches to trauma, helping you release what's held in your muscles, nervous system, and tissues. If physical symptoms accompany your emotional struggles, this approach may be especially helpful.

HOW TO FIND THE RIGHT PROFESSIONAL

Finding help can feel overwhelming when you're already struggling. Here are practical starting points:

- **Check your insurance provider's directory.** Most insurance companies maintain lists of covered mental health professionals. Filter by specialty if you're looking for trauma-informed care or a specific modality like EMDR.
- **Use the Psychology Today therapist directory.** This searchable database lets you filter by location, insurance, specialty, and treatment approach. Profiles include photos and descriptions so you can get a sense of fit before reaching out.
- **Ask your primary care physician for a referral.** Just as my doctor referred me to counseling services, yours can point you toward mental health support. They may know specialists in your area.
- **Contact your employer's Employee Assistance Program (EAP).** Many employers offer free confidential counseling sessions through EAP benefits. This can be a low-barrier way to start.
- **Look into community mental health centers.** If cost is a concern, community centers often offer sliding-scale fees based on income.
- **Ask for recommendations.** If you feel comfortable, ask trusted friends, family members, or your health coach if they know professionals they'd recommend.

WHAT TO EXPECT

The first appointment is usually an assessment—the professional gets to know you and your history, and you get to assess whether they feel like a good fit. It's okay to try a few therapists before finding the right one. The relationship matters. You deserve someone who sees you, respects your pace, and supports your healing.

Seeking help is not a sign that you've failed at self-care. It's a sign that you're taking your healing seriously. Some wounds need a professional guide. Your Authentic Self knows when it's time to reach out. Trust that knowing.

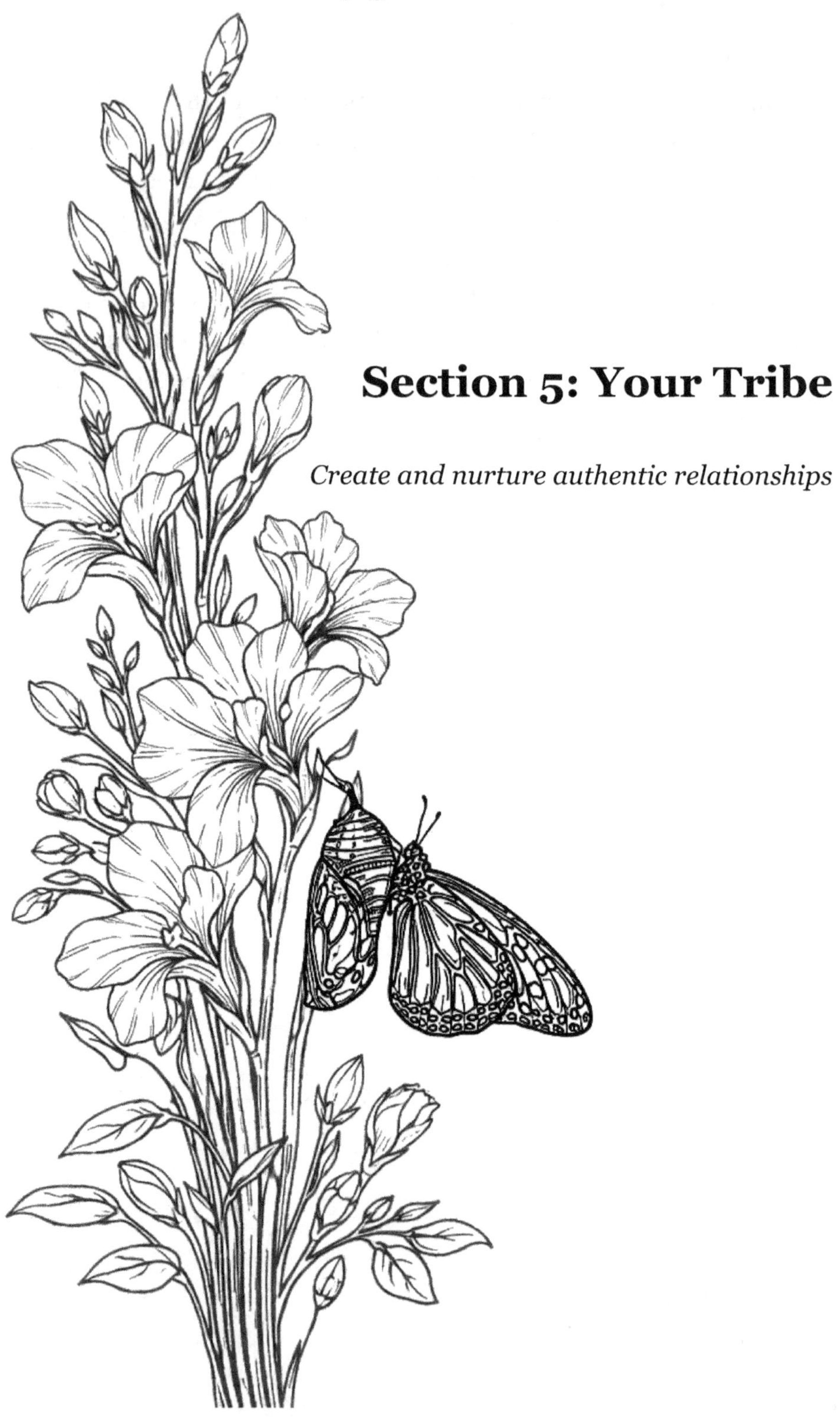

Section 5: Your Tribe

Create and nurture authentic relationships

Love Yourself First

Think of something you wish someone would do for you. Maybe it would be nice if someone bought you flowers, cooked you a meal, massaged your feet, or paid you a compliment. Why would you like someone to do these things? Because they bring you joy or make you feel special and loved. Now ask yourself: what's stopping you from doing these things for yourself?

Here's the truth we often forget—the actions and feelings of friends, family, and colleagues vary day to day. There's room for them to let you down. You can't rely on others for your happiness. The person most guaranteed to be there for you is you.

One day in 2017, I realized no one had ever bought me flowers. So I started buying myself a bouquet every week. I discovered roses were my favorite, but they were expensive. Then I drove past a rose gardening shop near my apartment and decided to check their prices. Each plant cost eighteen dollars—less than twice the price of a grocery store bouquet. I bought four plants. Years later, I have a potted rose garden, and I've named each plant. That initial step of self-love led to an ongoing joy.

When you show yourself love, your world looks brighter. And the brighter your world becomes, the easier it is to share your light and love with others. Your Authentic Self knows this truth: you cannot pour from an empty cup. Buy yourself roses. Cook yourself a meal from scratch. Get a foot massager. Write three things you appreciate about yourself each day. Whatever speaks to you, do it. You deserve your own love and attention.

If this feels uncomfortable—if giving yourself flowers or writing yourself compliments seems strange or self-indulgent—that's your Created Self talking. It learned that loving yourself means taking from others. Your Authentic Self knows differently: you can't give what you don't have. Filling your own cup isn't selfish. It's the foundation for everything else.

Intention of the Day
I will show myself love today so I remember I deserve care.

The Missing Ingredient in Love Languages

According to author Gary Chapman, the five love languages are Words of Affirmation, Acts of Service, Receiving Gifts, Quality Time, and Physical Touch. These languages help us understand how people prefer to give and receive love. But there's something this framework doesn't address—the energy behind those actions.

You can give someone a gift with genuine joy or bitter obligation. You can offer words of praise from true appreciation or from fear of conflict. You can do acts of service with care or resentment. Same action, completely different impact.

This is what I call Authentic Heart Energy. It's the emotional quality you bring to any expression of love. It's not a sixth love language. It's the foundation beneath all five that decides whether they nourish a relationship or slowly harm it.

Think about hugging your partner. If you're a "huggy" person, your embrace carries warmth and openness. But if you're not naturally affectionate and hug only because you feel you should, that reluctance comes through. Your partner receives the hug, but they also feel the resistance underneath it.

Or consider acts of service. You could clean the kitchen for your partner because you genuinely want to ease their burden—or because you're afraid of what happens if you don't. Same action. Completely different energy. And they feel the difference, even if they can't name it.

The love languages tell us what to do. Heart energy reveals who we're being while we do it. And who we're being matters far more than what we're doing.

When you bring awareness to your heart energy, you gain insight into the true health of your relationships. You can perform all five love languages perfectly and still create distance if your energy comes from fear, duty, or distraction instead of authentic connection.

Your Authentic Self knows the difference between love given freely and love performed out of obligation. Trust that knowing.

Intention of the Day:
I will pay attention to the energy I bring when I show love.

The Energy You Bring

Consider someone whose love language is acts of service, but their partner responds most to words of affirmation. They could offer compliments grudgingly, treating it like a chore they must perform to keep the peace. The words might be technically correct, but the heart energy behind them feels hollow.

Or they could see it as a chance to help their partner feel valued, speaking with genuine warmth. Same words, entirely different energy. The partner doesn't just hear the compliment—they feel whether it comes from duty or from care.

As you learned in "Understand Your Energy Body," you have an energy system that constantly interacts with the world around you. Heart energy is how that system shows up in your relationships—the emotional quality you bring to every interaction.

This matters because you can't fake heart energy. You might think you're hiding your resentment or anxiety, but it seeps into everything you offer. If you're acting from obligation, your partner will sense it even if they can't name what feels off.

Here's the truth: giving love from anything less than authentic connection—from fear of loss, from guilt, from habit—slowly erodes relationships. It's exhausting for you because you're wearing a mask. It's confusing for them because something feels wrong but they can't pinpoint what.

The path forward isn't to force better energy. It's to notice what you're actually feeling and get curious about it. Why does this feel like obligation instead of joy? What would need to shift for you to give this love authentically? Sometimes the answer is addressing something in the relationship. Sometimes it's recognizing you're trying to love in a way that doesn't fit who you are. And sometimes the answer is simply: I'm depleted. I need to fill my own cup before I can give to anyone else. That's not failure. That's honesty. Your tribe deserves your authentic energy—not your performance of it.

Your Authentic Self can't thrive when you're performing love you don't genuinely feel. Pay attention to the heart energy you bring. It's telling you something important about whether this relationship supports who you truly are.

Intention of the Day:
I will notice what heart energy I bring to my relationships today.

The Energy You Receive

Just as important as the heart energy you give is the heart energy you receive. Someone can perform all five love languages perfectly and still make you feel unsafe, uncomfortable, or like you need to shrink yourself.

Maybe your partner brings you gifts regularly, but there's an undercurrent of control in each one—like they're buying your compliance. Or they spend quality time with you, but their energy is distracted and impatient, making you feel like a burden. The action checks the box, but the energy underneath tells a different story.

Your Authentic Self can feel this, even when you can't articulate it. You might find yourself feeling anxious around someone who "does everything right." You might notice you're walking on eggshells with someone who's technically affectionate. That discomfort is data, not a defect in your perception.

If someone consistently brings energy that makes you uncomfortable—anxiety, criticism, possessiveness, resentment—you don't need to maintain that relationship just because they're going through the motions of love. The key is becoming aware of what energy you're accepting, so you don't stay in relationships that require you to betray your Authentic Self just to keep the peace.

Ask yourself: Does this person's presence make me feel safe, seen, and free to be myself? Or do I feel like I need to perform, apologize, or diminish who I am?

The relationships that truly feed your soul are the ones where the heart energy matches the loving actions. Trust your Authentic Self to recognize the difference. It knows which relationships nourish you and which ones ask you to abandon yourself.

Intention of the Day:
I will notice how I feel in the presence of those I love.

Your Tribe Is Self-Care

When I told my tribe I was having surgery, something remarkable happened. Without me asking, they offered to help. They knew I'm typically self-sufficient and independent—I rarely ask for support. But they showed up anyway. One offered to drive me to the hospital. Another volunteered to stay home with me overnight during recovery. Many brought meals. They didn't wait for me to request help. They simply showed up because that's what tribe does.

This experience reminded me of something crucial: building a tribe isn't optional. It's essential self-care.

Human beings are social by nature. Your thoughts, emotions, actions, and beliefs are all shaped by the people around you. This reality makes creating a network of people who make you feel loved, safe, and supported one of the most important investments you can make in your well-being.

Research confirms what your heart already knows. Studies by psychologist Julianne Holt-Lunstad found that weak social connection carries a health risk comparable to smoking fifteen cigarettes a day. Loneliness increases risk of heart disease, stroke, and early death. Connection isn't a luxury—it's a biological necessity. Your body and mind are designed for belonging.

WHAT MAKES SOMEONE TRIBE

Your tribe members are honest with you and allow you to be honest with them. Whether you're an introvert or extrovert, your tribe accepts you for exactly who you are. They encourage you to live authentically always. Your tribe feeds your soul with compassion and helps you navigate life's lessons at every turn.

Your tribe doesn't have to be large. Some people have dozens of close connections. Others have two or three people who truly see them. What matters isn't the number—it's the quality. Even one person who accepts you fully is enough to remind you that you belong.

The members of your tribe can include family, friends, neighbors, coworkers, teachers, and counselors. They fill different roles—nurturer, problem-solver, protector, playmate, motivator. Each member might be available at all times or have boundaries around when they show up. What matters is that they show up when you need them.

HOW TRIBE FORMS

You might wonder how to find these people. The truth is, tribe forms through many different pathways—some intentional, some completely unexpected.

Two of my closest tribe members came from graduate school. We developed our bond through shared interests like salsa dancing and cultural similarities. We weren't trying to build lifelong friendships—we were just enjoying each other's company. The depth came naturally over time.

Another tribe member came from Toastmasters International. We were both active participants, and we discovered a shared love of eating out at new restaurants. What started as a professional development activity became a genuine friendship built on curiosity and good food.

And then there's the most unlikely story. I met two tribe members at an airport when our connecting flights were cancelled. There were no hotel rooms available, so we spent the night together in a hotel lobby. Inconvenience became connection. Strangers became tribe.

These examples show something important: you don't have to force tribe-building. You have to show up—to activities, to interests, to moments—and let connection happen. Tribe forms when you're present and open, not when you're strategizing.

How to Build Your Tribe

If you're starting from scratch or rebuilding after loss or betrayal, these practices help:

Start with one person. You don't need a crowd. Identify one person in your life who feels safe—someone you trust, even a little. Invest in that relationship. Depth with one person matters more than surface connection with many.

Deepen before you widen. Before seeking new connections, look at existing ones. Is there an acquaintance who could become a friend? A colleague you enjoy but never see outside work? Sometimes tribe is already nearby, waiting to be nurtured.

Follow your genuine interests. Join activities you actually care about—not networking events designed to manufacture connection. Classes, volunteer work, spiritual communities, hobby groups, and clubs like Toastmasters put you alongside people who share your values. Shared interests create natural pathways to friendship.

Let trust build gradually. You can't rush authentic connection. Let relationships prove themselves over time. Notice who shows up consistently. Notice who asks about your life and remembers what you share. Notice who celebrates your wins and sits with you in your struggles. These are the markers of tribe.

Stay open to the unexpected. Some of your deepest connections may come from circumstances you didn't choose—a cancelled flight, a random seat assignment, a conversation in a waiting room. Stay present to the people around you. Tribe can show up anywhere.

When Building Tribe Feels Hard

Some obstacles make tribe-building feel impossible. Here's how to work with them:

"I'm introverted." Tribe doesn't require constant socializing. Introverts often prefer fewer, deeper connections—which is exactly what tribe is. You don't need a large social circle. You need a few people who truly know you. Quality time with one person counts.

"I've been betrayed before." Past hurt makes trusting again feel dangerous. This is wisdom, not weakness. Start small. Let people earn trust through consistent action over time. You don't have to open your whole heart immediately—you can offer it in increments as people prove themselves safe.

"I don't know where to find people." Look for spaces aligned with your values and interests: classes, volunteer organizations, spiritual communities, professional groups, online communities centered on shared passions. The goal isn't to find tribe directly—it's to put yourself in environments where tribe is likely to form.

"I'm new to this area." Geographic moves disrupt existing connections. Be patient with yourself. Seek out local versions of activities you enjoyed elsewhere. Accept that building tribe takes time, and feeling lonely during the transition doesn't mean you'll be lonely forever.

YOUR TRIBE IS WAITING

Your Authentic Self knows the difference between people who drain you and those who sustain you. Trust that knowing. Building your tribe is how you honor it.

The people who showed up for my surgery didn't appear overnight. Those relationships formed over years—through salsa dancing and Toastmasters and even a cancelled flight. I invested in them, and they invested in me. When I needed help, the foundation was already there.

Your tribe may already be forming. Stay present. Stay open. And trust that connection finds those who make room for it.

But as you build your tribe, you'll need to recognize something important: not every relationship that looks like tribe actually is tribe. Some relationships only function because someone is managing everyone's behavior. The next article helps you identify the difference— so you can invest your energy in connections that are genuinely authentic.

Intention of the Day
I will invest in relationships with people who support my Authentic Self.

When Connection Requires a Manager

My grandfather died when I was ten years old. Until that moment, my family had seemed to work well-everyone got along and gatherings felt pleasant. But his absence showed something I did not yet have words for: the family hadn't been held together by shared values. It had been held together by his presence.

Almost immediately, problems surfaced. People who had seemed happy to see each other started gossiping about each other. Anger that had been hidden came out. Behaviors my grandfather would never have tolerated became normal. I watched family bonds fall apart and could not understand why his death changed everything so fast. At the time, my Authentic Self felt the shift long before my mind understood it.

Years later, a graduate school workshop gave me the framework I needed. The workshop presenter explained the difference between a leader and a manager. A leader teaches the values to be upheld, guides by example, builds trust within the group, and creates a culture where those values persist even when the leader is absent. A manager teaches behavior, enforces behavior through judgement and consequences, and keeps order through their presence. When a leader is gone, the group continues to follow their example. When a manager is gone, the group misbehaves.

That's when I understood what happened to my family. My grandfather had been managing the family by demanding good behavior, shutting down conflict, and keeping everyone in line. He had set expectations without guidance on why those good behaviors mattered. He simply controlled the environment. The moment that control ended, so did the appearance of harmony.

When Relationships Are Led vs. Managed

This applies beyond family. It shows up in friendships, romantic bonds, and groups.

Managed relationships work only when someone insists on certain behavior. They require constant watching and fixing. Remove that person, and the problems surface.

Led relationships work because people share both values and a vision and they truly care about each other. Problems still arise, but people work through them together. The connection is real, not performed.

You can tell the difference by what happens during absence and conflict.

In managed relationships, absence may create sadness but also reveals problems. When the person keeping everyone in line is gone, anger surfaces and the bond falls apart. The harmony was just an act.

In led relationships, absence creates sadness but not destruction. People miss each other and may struggle, but the shared values remain.

In managed relationships, conflict gets shut down. Someone steps in to stop it or push for peace. Everyone learns to hide disagreement while anger festers.

In led relationships, conflict gets addressed. People feel safe being honest because the bond matters more than being right.

ARE YOU BEING MANAGED?

Your Authentic Self knows the difference between real connection and controlled performance. Here are signs you're in a managed relationship:

- You behave differently when a certain person is around. You're careful and controlled when they're present. When they leave, you relax—or the problems emerge.
- The relationship requires someone to always keep the peace. If that person stopped managing, everything would fall apart.
- Honesty feels risky. You can't share what you truly think because it would "cause problems."
- You feel relief when gatherings end—not normal tired, but true relief that you can stop performing.
- As you learned in "The Energy You Bring" and "The Energy You Receive," you can feel when something is off even when you can't name it. Managed relationships carry worry and control underneath pleasant surfaces.

ARE YOU THE MANAGER?

Sometimes you're the one doing the managing. This often happens when you grew up learning that stopping conflict was your job.

Signs you might be managing relationships:

- You feel responsible for everyone getting along and step in right away to fix conflict.
- You watch others' behavior constantly, always managing how they interact.
- Keeping relationships going feels like a full-time job that's draining you.
- You can't imagine what would happen if you stopped.

If this resonates, here's what your Authentic Self knows: it's not your job to control other people's behavior. As you learned in "Love Yourself First," you cannot pour from an empty cup. Managing everyone else leaves nothing for yourself.

WHAT AUTHENTIC CONNECTION LOOKS LIKE

Relationships that feed your soul don't require managing:

- People show up as themselves, with room for bad days and flaws.
- Conflict gets worked through, not shut down.
- Values persist because people truly care, not because someone's enforcing them.
- Everyone contributes to the group—no single person holds it together through force of will.

MOVING FORWARD

You alone can't change a managed relationship into a real one. True connection requires shared work. But you can stop playing the role of manager/managee by setting boundaries, refusing to manage others, and being honest about your feelings.

Some relationships were never built on a real foundation. Knowing this is valuable information about where your energy belongs.

As you'll learn in the next article, loving without fixing is one of the clearest ways to step out of a managed relationship and into real connection. Your Authentic Self deserves relationships where you don't have to perform to belong.

Intention of the Day
I will notice whether my relationships require managing or thrive through shared values.

Loving Without Fixing

In the previous article, you learned to recognize when you might be managing relationships—constantly monitoring others' behavior and keeping everyone in line. Now let's explore a specific form that managing often takes: trying to fix people you love.

If you grew up in chaos and unhappiness, you might have learned that fixing everything and making everyone happy is how you show love. For some, doing everything possible to remove chaos feels like the ultimate act of care. The problem is, this pattern can harm both you and the people you're trying to help.

This is your Created Self responding to childhood trauma. You learned that fixing problems keeps you safe and proves you care. But your Authentic Self knows the truth: you can't control what makes other people happy, and trying to do so depletes you.

When you try to fix everyone's problems, you spend enormous energy solving issues that aren't yours to solve. You might rob them of the chance to learn from their own challenges. Their struggles are meant to help them grow.

It's painful to accept that you can't fix someone you love, especially when you can see how their struggles hurt them. But here's what I've learned: when someone has made up their mind, the chances of changing it are slim. Save your energy for people who ask for help. The only time to push harder is when their decision will cause physical harm.

You can still offer help in healthy ways. Try Ask-Offer-Ask: First, ask if they're open to hearing your thoughts. If yes, offer your perspective briefly and without pressure. Then ask what they think about it. This respects their autonomy while showing you care. If they say no to your offer, honor that. Pushing after they've declined isn't love—it's control. For example: 'I noticed you mentioned struggling with your job search. Would you be open to hearing some thoughts I have?' If yes: 'I found this networking group really helpful when I was looking. Have you considered something like that?' Then: 'What do you think?' This respects their autonomy while showing you care.

You can love someone, be there for them, and let them know you care—without taking on their problems as your own. That's not abandoning them. That's respecting their journey while protecting your own well-being. Everyone has the right to make their own choices, even mistakes. Your role is to love them, not fix them.

Intention of the Day
I will offer help respectfully and honor others' right to decline it.

When Caring Becomes Depleting

In the previous article, you learned that loving someone doesn't mean fixing them, but what happens when you've spent years absorbing everyone else's pain and prioritizing everyone else's needs? What happens when caring for others becomes the thing that's breaking you?

This is compassion fatigue—and it's different from ordinary burnout.

WHAT COMPASSION FATIGUE REALLY IS

Burnout comes from working too hard or doing too much, but compassion fatigue comes specifically from caring for others. It's what happens when you absorb the emotional weight of other people's struggles until you have nothing left for yourself.

Health professionals, caregivers, and teachers know this exhaustion well, but you don't need a caregiving profession to experience it. If you're the friend everyone calls in crisis or the family member who solves everyone's problems, you're vulnerable too.

I know this firsthand as a full-time health coach, holding space for clients' struggles with chronic illness, grief, and life transitions. I'm also a part-time energy healer, working with people's emotional and physical pain, and I pet-sit for friends because I genuinely love their animals. I support my friends and family through their challenges and stay active in my community. Each of these roles matters to me and feeds my purpose.

But here's what I've learned: when you care deeply about many people across many contexts, the cumulative weight becomes more than you realize, and compassion fatigue creeps in quietly until one day you're completely depleted.

How Compassion Fatigue Shows Up

Unlike burnout, which you can trace to overwork, compassion fatigue affects your ability to feel in distinct ways:

Emotional numbness. You used to feel moved by others' stories, but now you feel nothing—or worse, annoyed by their needs because your emotional reserves are empty.

Physical exhaustion that sleep doesn't fix. Your body is processing not just your own stress but the emotional weight you've absorbed from others.

Resentment—followed by guilt. This is the cycle I know well: someone asks for help and you feel resentment rise up, then immediately guilt floods in. You think: *I'm a terrible person. I should want to help. What's wrong with me?* Nothing is wrong with you—resentment is your body's warning signal that you've exceeded your capacity, and the guilt comes from your Created Self insisting that caring people never say no. Your Authentic Self knows the truth: resentment means you've already given too much.

Absorbing others' emotions as your own. You carry their anxiety, grief, and fear long after the conversation ends, taking on energy that isn't yours to hold, as you learned in "The Energy You Receive."

Cynicism about helping. You used to find meaning in supporting others, but now it feels pointless or frustrating—a shift that signals you've given more than you had to give.

THE CREATED SELF'S ROLE

Your Created Self learned that your worth depends on how much you give—perhaps you were praised for being helpful, learned other people's needs always come first, or discovered that managing everyone's emotions kept your environment safe. These patterns made sense when they formed, but they're not sustainable forever.

Your Authentic Self knows the difference between caring and depleting yourself, understanding that you can't pour from an empty cup—a truth you explored in "The Impossibility of Pleasing Everyone." Protecting your capacity isn't selfish; it's how you sustain your ability to care.

WHY THIS MATTERS NOW

If you recognize yourself in these patterns, you might wonder: Does this mean I should stop caring?

No. Compassion fatigue doesn't mean caring is wrong. It means the way you've been caring isn't sustainable.

Think about airplane safety instructions. Flight attendants tell you to put your oxygen mask on first before helping others. Not because you matter more—because if you pass out from lack of oxygen, you can't help anyone.

Compassion fatigue is your body telling you: you're running out of oxygen. You need to put your mask on before you collapse.

CARING WITHOUT ABSORBING

Sustainable caring requires boundaries:

Compassion with boundaries. You can care deeply without taking on their pain as your own. You can listen without fixing, witness without absorbing. As you learned in "Loving Without Fixing," honoring someone's autonomy is an act of love.

Know your limits. Remember "Know Your Limits Before You Cross Them"? Those limits apply to emotional labor too. You can only hold space for so many people before your capacity runs out.

Separate your feelings from theirs. When you carry someone's anxiety hours after talking with them, pause. Ask: Is this mine, or did I take it from them? Release what isn't yours to carry.

Rest as essential, not optional. As you learned in "Take a Break," rest isn't earned through suffering. Your nervous system needs time to recover from the emotional weight you've been carrying.

Say no without guilt. When experiencing compassion fatigue, saying no isn't just a boundary—it's survival. You can care about someone and still tell them you don't have capacity right now.

WHEN PROFESSIONAL SUPPORT HELPS

If you're in a caregiving profession—health coach, therapist, nurse, social worker, teacher, energy healer—compassion fatigue is an occupational hazard. Many professions offer supervision or peer support groups focused on preventing and recovering from compassion fatigue. Seek these out.

If you're experiencing severe symptoms—complete emotional shutdown, chronic illness, inability to function—please seek support from a mental health professional. As you learned in "Self-Care Tip: When to Seek Professional Help," recognizing when you need more than self-care is wisdom, not weakness.

YOUR TRIBE NEEDS YOU WHOLE

In "Your Tribe is Self-Care," you learned that connection is essential. But here's the truth: your tribe needs you healthy more than they need you exhausted.

The people who genuinely care about you don't want you depleted. They want you thriving. If someone demands that you sacrifice your well-being to meet their needs, they're not asking for care—they're asking for control. As you learned in "When Connection Requires a Manager," relationships built on one person's constant sacrifice aren't sustainable.

Your Authentic Self knows this: caring for yourself isn't selfish when you've been caring for everyone else. It's how you survive. It's how you keep showing up.

You are allowed to rest. You are allowed to set boundaries. You are allowed to protect your emotional energy. These aren't betrayals of the people you love—they're how you stay present for them long-term.

Intention of the Day
I will notice when caring depletes me and protect my capacity.

Your Tribe Evolves with You

The tribe that supported you five years ago might look different from the tribe you need today. This isn't failure—it's growth.

As you evolve and connect more deeply with your Authentic Self, your needs change. The friend who was perfect for late-night adventures in your twenties might not be the person you need when you're navigating a career change in your thirties. The colleague who energized you at your old job might drain you in your new role. The family member who once felt safe might no longer honor who you're becoming.

This shift can feel uncomfortable. You might worry that letting someone drift from your inner circle means you're being disloyal or ungrateful. But your Authentic Self knows better. Outgrowing a relationship doesn't diminish what that person once meant to you. It simply acknowledges that you've both changed, and what you need now is different from what you needed then.

Some tribe members will grow with you. They'll adapt as you evolve, and your connection will deepen over time. Others will naturally fall away, and that's okay. Making space for new people who fit who you're becoming honors both your journey and theirs.

You and your best friend from college may evolve together—your conversations deepen, your support strengthens, your connection matures. Or you may drift naturally apart as your lives take different directions. Neither outcome is wrong. What matters is honoring the truth of where you actually are, not where you wish you were or where you used to be.

Your tribe should always serve your highest good. When someone no longer supports your Authentic Self—when interactions leave you drained rather than nourished—it's time to reconsider their place in your inner circle. This doesn't require drama or confrontation. Sometimes it's simply about creating distance and redirecting your energy toward relationships that truly sustain you. Trust that your tribe will shift as you do. The people meant to walk alongside you will make themselves known.

Intention of the Day
I will notice which relationships sustain me and which ones drain me.

Know Your Tribe

As your tribe evolves, you may discover something surprising: some of your closest family members aren't related to you at all.

When my neighbor's dog died, he worried people would judge him for grieving so deeply. I asked him four questions: "Did your dog love you?" "Was he always happy to see you?" "Would he have risked his life to protect you?" "Did he accept you for who you are?"

He said yes to all of them.

"How many relatives can you say the same about?"

"Wow!" The look on his face shifted from grief to understanding. His dog wasn't just a pet. His dog was family—not because of biology, but because of unconditional love and acceptance.

This is the truth your Authentic Self already knows: family isn't determined by blood. It's determined by who shows up for you, who celebrates you, and who stays even when things get hard. Your family loves you through thick and thin, accepts you as you are, and adds to the quality of your life. They might be friends, neighbors, coworkers, or mentors. If you're lucky, some of your relatives become family too.

Our relatives are the first community we receive. By interacting with them during our youth, we learn what we value in relationships and how we want to be treated. They serve as teachers—even the difficult ones—helping us recognize what we truly need from our chosen family.

Be grateful for those lessons, even from relatives you've had to release. And nurture the bonds with those who've earned the title of family. You've already invested your heart in choosing them.

Intention of the Day
I will show up for my chosen family, because my chosen family shows up for me.

Be Mindful of Your Words

Your tribe sustains you—and communication is how you build and maintain those bonds. The next four articles focus on how to speak and listen in ways that strengthen rather than strain your relationships.

When you tell someone "I like your shirt," what's behind it? Do you actually like the shirt? Are you just being polite? Or are you being sarcastic, hoping to make them second-guess their choice? The words are the same. The intention changes everything.

Words carry more than their surface meaning. They carry the emotions and intentions of the person speaking them. A compliment given with genuine warmth lands differently than one offered out of obligation. A question asked with curiosity feels different from one laced with judgment. People sense the difference, even when they can't name it.

Here's what makes this matter: the impact of your words doesn't stop with the person you're talking to. When your words uplift someone, they carry that energy into their next interaction. When your words wound or dismiss, that hurt travels too. The cashier you snapped at may snap at the next customer. The friend you encouraged may encourage someone else. Your words create ripples you'll never see.

This is especially important with your tribe—the people you interact with most frequently. With them, your words build up over time. The partner you dismiss today may withdraw a little more each time. The friend you encourage regularly becomes more resilient. With your tribe, every word is both immediate impact and ongoing investment.

This is why mindfulness matters. Before you speak, pause. Ask yourself: What is my intention here? Am I trying to connect, or am I trying to control? Am I adding to this person's day, or subtracting from it? Your Authentic Self speaks to build up, clarify, and connect. Your Created Self sometimes speaks to protect, impress, or wound.

You can't take words back once they're spoken. But you can choose them with care. Every conversation is a chance to add something good to the world—or to take something away. Choose wisely.

Intention of the Day
I will speak with intention so my words add to someone's day.

Speaking Well

The previous article explored how your words affect others. This one is about how your words affect you.

Every word you speak—aloud or in your mind—adds to or subtracts from your own energy. When something annoys you, do the words of irritation you mutter or think make you feel better? Or do they feed the annoyance, making it grow?

Think of it like a snowball rolling downhill. In cartoons, it gathers more snow and becomes a boulder. Negativity works the same way. When you complain, criticize, or speak harshly—even to yourself—you feed the negativity you're carrying. It doesn't matter where the words are directed. They still affect you.

This is especially true of self-talk. The words you say to yourself in your own mind shape how you feel. "I'm so stupid" lands in your body. "I can't do anything right" becomes a weight you carry. Your Created Self often speaks this way—echoing old criticisms, rehearsing fears, predicting failure. But these words aren't neutral. They cost you energy and peace.

Your Authentic Self speaks differently. It offers patience instead of judgment. It says "I'm learning" instead of "I'm failing." It chooses words that support rather than tear down. The way you speak to yourself affects how you show up for your tribe. Self-criticism depletes the energy you have for connection. Self-compassion preserves it. When you treat yourself with kindness internally, you have more capacity to show up with genuine presence for the people who matter to you.

Here's the practice: when negativity comes your way—from others or from your own mind—try to combat it with positive words. Not fake cheerfulness, but genuine reframing. Instead of "This is terrible," try "This is hard, and I can handle hard things." Instead of "I always mess up," try "I'm doing my best today."

The words you speak to yourself matter. Choose ones that serve your peace.

Intention of the Day
I will combat negativity today with words that serve my peace.

Share Your Concerns

Have you ever held back from expressing what's bothering you because you didn't want to seem like a complainer? You're not alone. Many of us learned that voicing distress makes us burdensome or negative. But here's what that lesson misses: expressing grief, pain, or discontent is a natural human need.

Think about it. Saying "my broken leg hurts" is technically a complaint. So is "the AC hasn't worked in days." These are completely reasonable expressions of distress. The problem isn't the act of sharing your concerns—it's the intention behind it.

Your Authentic Self shares concerns to seek help, find solutions, or gain perspective from someone who cares. There's an openness to change, a desire for resolution or connection. This kind of expression strengthens relationships because it invites others into your experience and allows them to support you.

But sometimes we fall into a different pattern. When we're overwhelmed or stuck, we might vent the same frustrations repeatedly without seeking resolution. We're not looking for help—we're looking for someone to agree that we're right to feel upset. This pattern drains both you and your listener. It keeps you stuck in the problem rather than moving toward relief.

The difference isn't whether you express distress. It's whether you're open to something shifting when you do.

Before sharing a concern, pause and notice your intention. Are you seeking support, clarity, or a solution? Or are you seeking agreement for a position you've already locked into? When your intent is genuine connection or resolution, the people who know you will listen and help every time.

If you worry that you're burdening your tribe, remember: they want to support you. That's what tribe does. The difference between healthy sharing and overwhelming someone is your openness to their response. If you share hoping they'll help you see differently, that's connection. If you share demanding they agree you're right to stay stuck, that's draining.

Trust your people to tell you if they can't hold space right now—and honor that boundary when they do.

Intention of the Day
I will share one concern today with openness to support, perspective, or resolution.

Healing through Listening

In "Share Your Concerns," we explored how expressing your struggles can strengthen relationships. But what about the other side—when someone shares with you?

Here's what most people get wrong: they think listening means solving. Someone shares a problem, and you immediately start troubleshooting. But often, people don't need you to fix anything. They need to be heard.

I learned this from my therapist during graduate school. My mind was so loud with stress and uncertainty that I felt like I was going insane. When I sat with him, he didn't rush to give advice or solve my problems. He simply listened with full attention. That feeling of being truly heard settled my mind enough to start thinking clearly again. The noise quieted. I could finally troubleshoot my own next steps.

This is the healing power of listening. When you give someone your full presence—not distracted, not preparing your response, not judging— you create space for them to release what they're carrying. Your care allows them to make room for peace. You don't have to have answers. Your attention is the gift.

And listening benefits you too. You learn more about the person sharing. You see how experiences you've never had can affect someone. You practice being present without needing to control or fix. This is your Authentic Self showing up—connected, compassionate, and calm.

Listening to someone's struggles doesn't have to be heavy or draining. When you release the pressure to solve, it becomes an act of love. Your presence alone can bring healing.

How to listen: Put your phone away. Make eye contact. Don't interrupt to share your own story. Don't rush to fix or advise. When they pause, wait three seconds before responding—they may have more to say. Sometimes the most healing thing you can offer is: 'I'm here. I'm listening. You're not alone.

Intention of the Day
I will listen with care so someone feels less alone today.

Section 6: Your Purpose

Live with intention and meaning

Lessons in the Negative

You've learned how to build and nurture authentic relationships. Now comes a different question: what are you here to do with your life? Purpose isn't about your tribe—it's about how your Authentic Self shows up in the world. And often, purpose clarifies itself not through ease, but through adversity.

When your work stops working—when the career you built stalls, the business you started struggles, or the path you chose feels wrong—a choice emerges. You can spend your energy resenting the difficulty, or redirect that energy toward discovering what this crisis is trying to teach you about your purpose.

It's natural to feel discouraged when life isn't working. You might spend days or weeks cycling through frustration, sadness, or despair. That's human. But at some point, a choice emerges: Will you keep pouring energy into how bad things are, or will you redirect that energy toward change?

I faced this choice when the pandemic hit my business. I had started My Wealth in Health in May 2019. By January 2020, I had coaching and Reiki clients every day and had just taught my first class of six students. Everything was falling into place—and my business wasn't even a year old. Then social distancing put it in a chokehold—from daily clients to two per month for six months. Meanwhile, large companies began offering free coaching as an employee benefit. New coaches with private practices didn't stand a chance.

I saw this as a test—you might call it the Universe testing me, or simply circumstances revealing my priorities. Either way, the question was the same: was I sure this was part of my life purpose? Your Created Self has two responses to crisis: give up immediately, or push through no matter the cost. Both ignore the real question. Your Authentic Self asks something different: 'Is this challenge revealing that this work matters enough to fight for—or that it was never mine to begin with?' I took stock: my overhead was low, so closing wasn't necessary yet. I took a full-time coaching job to stay afloat. Then I used the downtime to learn search engine optimization and expand my Reiki training. By the time people felt safe to return, I was easier to find on Google, ready to teach online, and had more techniques at my disposal.

So, Universe, the answer is yes. That clarity came from adversity. If coaching and energy healing had just been comfortable jobs, the pandemic might have made me quit. But these aren't jobs—they're how my Authentic Self serves the world. The test revealed that truth.

Every difficult situation contains something useful—if you're willing to look. Your Authentic Self knows that growth often comes from difficulty. Trust that even this experience has something to give you.

Intention of the Day
I will find one lesson in a negative situation today.

Self-Care Tip: Volunteer

How do you discover what you're meant to do? Sometimes the answer emerges not through introspection but through action—specifically, through serving others.

Volunteering offers a low-risk way to explore what lights you up. Unlike a career change, volunteering lets you test different forms of service without commitment. You might discover that working with animals brings you alive, or that mentoring young people connects you to something deeper, or that organizing community events reveals skills you didn't know you had. Each experience teaches you something about your Authentic Self.

I used to volunteer at the local animal shelter walking dogs. Many were skittish and fearful. I remember Bitzy, a small black dog who wouldn't even stand the first time I took her out. I had to carry her away from the barking to get her to walk. The second time, she was more confident with her tail up. By the third walk, her ears stood straight and her tail wagged when she saw me. She was adopted soon after. I was so happy to see her come out of her shell—I almost adopted her myself. Those moments with the dogs helped me forget about the troubles of the world—but more than that, they showed me how much I value witnessing transformation. That insight shaped the healing work I do today.

Volunteering isn't just about giving—it also fills your own cup. It provides perspective on your own challenges and reminds you what truly matters. When you help others, you experience the fulfillment that comes from making a difference. That fulfillment is data: it's your Authentic Self telling you something about your purpose.

There are so many needs in a community that can be met with just an extra pair of hands. Walking dogs at an animal shelter. Mowing the lawn for a disabled homeowner. Taking the trash to the curb for an elderly neighbor who struggles to lift it. Organizing charity events. Working as a receptionist at a free clinic. Mentoring in an afterschool program. Each builds skills while serving others—and each reveals something about what kind of service calls to your soul.

Not sure you'll have time? Some employers offer volunteer paid time off through employee assistance programs, letting you volunteer during work hours. Check with your HR department.

You can find opportunities through VolunteerMatch.org, local nonprofits, community centers, or places of worship. Even five minutes a week makes a meaningful difference—and might show you something important about who you're meant to become.

Step Out of Your Comfort Zone

You've learned that adversity can clarify your purpose. But sometimes discovering what truly lights you up requires stepping into experiences you'd never choose on your own. Your Authentic Self contains capacities and values you haven't discovered yet—qualities your purpose will need—because you simply haven't tried the things that would reveal them.

One night during my third year of college, some friends knocked on my dorm room door shouting, "We're going country line dancing! Let's go!" What would make a Jamaican go country line dancing in Connecticut? Friends offering to pay for everything.

For two hours straight, I sat at our table at this huge dance club refusing to help my friends mess up the dance floor formation. They had no clue what they were doing but were having tons of fun. I, on the other hand, didn't want to embarrass myself.

Just when I became bored, I noticed there was a mechanical bull at the back of the dance floor. Eager to harness my inner John Travolta in "Urban Cowboy," I ran over to the mechanical bull, paid the operator, and held on for dear life. While riding the bull, the operator increased the speed every eight seconds. About thirty seconds in, people started cheering me on. I lasted just over a minute before I fell off the mechanical bull to a burst of applause. The operator then told me most people don't usually last as long on the mechanical bull as I did.

Not only did I have fun; I also felt a sense of achievement! I was as happy as can be and that glee finally took me to the dance floor to join my friends. I enjoyed country line dancing so much that my friends had to wait on me to end the night. Five years later, I knew all the popular country line dances; got to the second-highest speed allowed in clubs on the mechanical bull; and proudly owned three cowboy hats, two belt buckles, cowboy boots, cowboy boot shoes, and a bolo tie. A couple of my friends even nicknamed me the Jamaican Hillbilly!

The Created Self would have kept me sitting at that table all night. It insisted that trying something new meant risking embarrassment, that I should already know how to dance before attempting it, that people would judge me. Your Authentic Self doesn't care about looking foolish— it cares about being alive. When you listen to it, experiences you'd never choose become the ones that change you.

If I hadn't gone out with my friends that night in 2002, I never would have discovered the joy of country line dancing. That one spontaneous night revealed a creative, playful side of my Authentic Self I didn't know existed.

Country line dancing isn't my life's purpose—coaching and energy healing are. But that spontaneous yes taught me something crucial about discovering purpose: your Authentic Self reveals itself through joy. When you try something new and feel completely alive doing it, you've discovered a quality of your Authentic Self. For me, country dancing revealed playfulness, physical expression, and love of community. Those same qualities show up in how I teach Reiki, lead workshops, and create space for clients to heal. The activity that sparked the joy wasn't the purpose—but the joy itself pointed toward what my purpose needed to include.

Your purpose isn't always hiding in the "logical" places. Sometimes you discover what makes you come alive by saying "yes" to experiences that seem to have nothing to do with your plan. The mechanical bull had nothing to do with my biology degree or my future career—but it taught me I'm braver than I thought, and that joy often lives on the other side of fear.

Purpose isn't the same as hobby. Country line dancing brings me joy, but coaching and energy healing are my purpose—they're how my Authentic Self serves others and expresses what I value most. Yet discovering that playful, embodied part of myself through dancing shaped how I approach my purpose work. Exploration doesn't always lead directly to purpose, but it always reveals qualities of your Authentic Self that your purpose needs to include.

Those discoveries matter when you're building a life that's authentically yours. Your purpose reveals itself not through careful planning, but through following what makes you feel alive—even when it comes from the most unexpected places.

Intention of the Day
I will step outside my comfort zone to discover hidden parts of myself.

Self-Care Tip: Explore

There may be parts of your Authentic Self that are yet to be discovered. This happens because you haven't had the experiences that would reveal them. Repeating the same routine day after day robs you of those opportunities. Don't wait for new experiences to come to you. Go to them.

A friend once asked me to visit a lavender farm with her. It was out in the country, and I was skeptical about going. On the drive, I worried we were heading into the middle of nowhere and regretted agreeing to the trip. But when we arrived, the farm was breathtaking—rows upon rows of lush lavender plants in different varieties, stretching out before us.

The farm was hosting a festival that highlighted the many uses of lavender. There were workshops on tucking dried lavender into sachets, making door wreaths and crowns from the stems and flowers, and blending essential oils. A shop on the grounds sold soaps, lotions, and creams made from lavender. The farm even had donkeys and chickens for children to pet, plus a small flower garden for picnics and quiet walks.

I learned so much that day. Now I imagine my dream home with potted lavender plants by the front and back doors—beautiful and practical for deterring mosquitoes. That single trip revealed a part of myself I hadn't known: someone who finds peace and restoration in farms and gardens. Since then, I look for opportunities to return.

Exploration doesn't require traveling far. Take a painting workshop, tour a brewery, visit a local festival, or try a new hiking trail. What matters is that you make it something new. Stepping out of your comfort zone is how your Authentic Self reveals itself.

Make Your Dreams a Reality

You've tested your purpose through adversity. You've explored new experiences that revealed hidden strengths. But discovery isn't enough. At some point, your Authentic Self asks you to move from understanding your purpose to actually living it. That's when fear shows up—and fear doesn't always mean stop.

Human beings constantly exceed their own expectations. We have cured diseases, visited the moon, and split atoms. Gene Roddenberry imagined communicators, PADDs, and replicators for Star Trek in 1966. Now we have smartphones, tablets, and 3D printers. Everything we have today was once just an idea, dream, or fantasy.

But here's what matters for your individual purpose: those technological breakthroughs happened because the people pursuing them weren't just chasing achievement. Gene Roddenberry imagined technology that served human connection. Engineers built smartphones because communication mattered to them, not just because it was technically possible. When innovation aligns with authentic purpose—with what you genuinely value—it becomes sustainable. When it's just ambition, burnout follows.

This capacity for achievement lives in you too. But here's what matters: the dream must be authentically yours.

Here's the difference: your Created Self dreams about what will earn approval, status, or security. It chases achievements that look impressive from the outside. Your Authentic Self dreams about what allows you to express who you truly are—whether or not anyone applauds. Becoming wealthy can be either, depending on why you want it. Building a business can be either, depending on what you're building and who it serves. The dream itself isn't the question. The question is: whose dream is this?

When you pursue goals inherited from family, culture, or society's expectations, you're working against your own grain. Progress feels like pushing a boulder uphill. But when you pursue what your Authentic Self truly desires, something shifts. Possibilities become limitless because you're aligned with who you really are.

How do you know the difference? Pay attention to overwhelm—but understand what it's telling you.

Sometimes overwhelm signals that a dream is deeply meaningful. It matters so much that the scope feels daunting. The size of your fear matches the size of what you're reaching for. This overwhelm says, "This is important. Proceed with care."

Other times, overwhelm signals misalignment. You're chasing something that was never yours to begin with—a parent's dream, society's expectation, an image of who you "should" be. This overwhelm says, "This doesn't fit. Let it go."

Your Authentic Self knows which is which. The meaningful dream pulls you forward even when you're scared. The misaligned dream just weighs you down. Trust that knowing. I've experienced this firsthand. When I decided to write this book, the idea was overwhelming. But I knew there was an audience who would benefit from it. That knowing kept me going since 2021. The overwhelm didn't mean I should stop—it meant the dream mattered enough to feel big.

Your purpose might not look like writing a book or building a business. It might be creating a home where foster children feel safe. It might be mastering a craft that brings beauty into the world. It might be showing up consistently for people others have written off. The scale doesn't matter. What matters is that the dream is authentically yours— that it lets your Authentic Self express itself in the world.

Whatever dream calls to your soul, trust that humans have always turned imagination into reality. You carry that same capacity. The question isn't whether you're capable. It's whether the dream is authentically yours.

Intention of the Day
I will take one step toward a dream that is authentically mine.

From Idea to Action

You have a dream that's authentically yours—whether you've just confirmed that by working through the previous article, or you've known it in your bones for years. The vision is clear; the desire is real. Now comes the practical question: how do you move from idea to reality?

Start by remembering: you don't have to do it alone.

First, know that the idea doesn't have to come from you alone. Some of the greatest achievements in history came from collaboration—groups of people working toward the same goal, each contributing what they could. If you need help brainstorming, reach out to people you trust who can honor your values while helping you think through possibilities. Asking for support isn't weakness. It's wisdom.

Your Created Self insists you should have all the answers before you begin, that needing help means you're not qualified for this dream. Your Authentic Self knows that meaningful work rarely happens alone—and that the right collaborators amplify rather than diminish your vision.

When overwhelm hits, it's often because the whole feels too big to hold. Not all overwhelm means the same thing. Sometimes overwhelm signals that you're pursuing the wrong dream—one that belongs to your Created Self's need for approval rather than your Authentic Self's genuine purpose. That kind of overwhelm tells you to stop and reassess.

But if you've already determined this dream is authentically yours, the overwhelm you're feeling now is different. It comes from seeing the size of something that genuinely matters. It's not telling you the dream is wrong—it's telling you that you're trying to see the entire staircase when all you need is the next step. When you break the dream into smaller questions, the overwhelm shifts from paralyzing to manageable. Break it down. Ask yourself these questions:

- Why does it matter to me?
- What does success look like?
- How will I take the first step?
- Who can help me get there?
- Where can I find the resources I need?
- When is the best time to act?

You don't need to answer all of these at once. Start with one. Then another. Each answer builds momentum. For example, when I launched My Wealth in Health, "Why?" gave me clarity to support people's authentic self-care. "What does success look like?" meant defining my

144

services clearly. "How do I take the first step?" was getting my first client. "Who can help?" led me to other health coaches, business mentors, and supportive friends. Each question moved the dream from overwhelming to achievable.

It's common to have an idea and not follow through—not because you lack ability, but because the path forward feels unclear. Here's what many people miss: Clarity comes from movement, not from waiting until everything is figured out. You can't see the next step until you take the current one; action creates information that planning alone never provides.

You've already created meaningful things in your life—relationships, solutions to problems, moments of beauty. This dream is just the next expression of that same capacity. History shows that humans turn imagination into reality. You carry that same capacity. The path reveals itself as you walk it—one question, one answer, one step at a time. The dream is yours. Now make it real.

Intention of the Day
I will answer one question that moves my dream closer to reality.

Fearlessness Is Your Birthright

You've identified your authentic purpose. You've broken it down into actionable steps. Now fear shows up. It makes sense—pursuing your purpose means risking failure, judgment, rejection. When you've been hurt before, staying small can feel like the safest option. Please don't judge yourself for feeling afraid. The question isn't whether fear will show up. It's whether you'll let it stop you.

And yet—fear can also keep you frozen in situations that slowly drain your life force. The toxic relationship. The dead-end job. The life that no longer fits. You might know exactly what needs to change, but fear of the unknown keeps you patching a wound that won't heal while the source of pain remains.

Sometimes fearlessness means stepping into the unknown to discover who you are—like my trip to Rome. Other times it means stepping away from the familiar because it's destroying who you're meant to become. Both require the same capacity: trusting yourself to handle what comes next, even when you can't see the entire path.

Here's what I want you to remember: fearlessness doesn't mean never feeling afraid. It means trusting yourself to move forward even when fear is present. That trust comes from evidence—evidence that you've navigated challenges before, that you can read situations accurately, that you know the difference between intuition warning you of real danger and anxiety trying to keep you comfortable. Fearlessness is your birthright because you carry the same capacity that enabled humans to leave familiar territory and build extraordinary things. Your ancestors took enormous risks to survive and thrive. That courage lives in you.

In July 2009, I traveled to Rome alone for a conference. My family begged me not to go—a Black woman from Jamaica traveling solo felt too risky to them. This is how Created Self operates—in you and in the people who love you. It scans for danger, amplifies worst-case scenarios, and insists that safety requires staying small. Your Authentic Self knows something different: some risks are worth taking. Some experiences matter more than the comfort of staying home. My family's Created Self saw danger. My Authentic Self saw growth. But I went anyway. I presented my research, then spent my free time wandering ancient streets. I found the best pizza and gelato of my life at tiny shops with no signs. I walked through ruins that had stood for thousands of years. For the first time in my life, I felt complete mental peace. I moved through each day in pure presence, making every choice for myself alone. No one else's fears. No one else's expectations. Just me. I came home safely, changed by what I'd chosen to risk.

That trip taught me something essential about purpose: fear doesn't mean stop. When my family worried about my solo travel, they weren't wrong to be concerned—solo travel carries real risks. But their fears were based on worst-case scenarios, not on who I actually am or what I can handle. The same is true when you pursue your purpose. People will project their fears onto your dreams. They'll tell you it's too risky, too uncertain, too much. Sometimes those fears reflect their own limitations, not yours. Fearlessness isn't ignoring real dangers—it's distinguishing between actual risks and projected anxieties. Your purpose is worth the real risk.

That trip taught me something: fearlessness runs in your DNA. When early humans first left Africa thousands of years ago, they walked into territories no one had ever seen. We watched birds fly and decided we could too. We built the first airplane, then landed on the moon. Every major leap forward required choosing the unknown over the familiar. That same courage lives in you—even when fear tries to convince you otherwise.

I've needed that same fearlessness to pursue my purpose. Starting My Wealth in Health meant risking financial stability. Teaching Reiki workshops meant risking judgment from people who don't believe in energy healing. Writing this book meant risking vulnerability—sharing my struggles publicly. Each time, fear showed up. Each time, I chose to move forward anyway, not because the fear disappeared, but because my purpose mattered more than my comfort.

Fearlessness doesn't mean ignoring real dangers or pretending you're not scared. It means trusting yourself to face the unknown in pursuit of your purpose—in pursuit of what your Authentic Self is here to do. You get to decide which risks serve your purpose and which don't. And you get to move at your own pace. But don't let fear convince you that staying safe means staying small.

Intention of the Day
I will trust myself to navigate the unknown so I can live freely.

Recognizing Your Created Self at Work

Not everyone's purpose lives at work. For many people, work is how they pay bills while pursuing purpose elsewhere—through relationships, creativity, service, or personal growth. But work takes up the majority of your waking hours. This creates a critical challenge: if work drains your Authentic Self completely, you'll have nothing left for the purpose that actually matters to you.

If your work IS your purpose—if your job aligns with your Authentic Self—some of what follows may not apply to you. But even purpose-aligned work happens within workplace cultures that can pressure you to perform rather than be real. Whether your job is your purpose or simply funds it, recognizing when your Created Self takes over is the first step toward protecting yourself.

Work has a way of pulling your Created Self to the surface. The pressure to perform, fit in, and prove your value can override what you actually think, feel, and need. Before you realize it, you've abandoned yourself to meet expectations that may not even be yours.

This happens because workplaces often reward the Created Self. You learn quickly what earns approval: staying late, saying yes, keeping opinions to yourself, adapting your personality to match the culture. These changes help you survive professionally—but they come at a cost your Authentic Self eventually pays.

RECOGNIZING CREATED SELF PATTERNS AT WORK

Notice if any of these patterns feel familiar:

Overworking to prove worth or avoid judgment. You stay late not because the work requires it, but because you fear what others will think if you leave on time. Your value feels tied to visible effort rather than actual contribution.

Saying yes to requests that violate your limits. A colleague asks for help when you're already overwhelmed. Your manager adds another project to your full plate. You say yes because no feels too risky—even when yes costs you sleep, health, or sanity.

Silencing your opinions in meetings to avoid conflict. You have thoughts, ideas, and concerns. But you've learned that speaking up leads to pushback, dismissal, or being labeled difficult. So you stay quiet and watch decisions unfold that you could have improved.

Adapting your personality to fit workplace culture. You become a different version of yourself at work—more agreeable, less expressive, carefully curated. The person your colleagues know isn't quite the person you actually are.

Taking on others' responsibilities to be seen as a team player. You absorb tasks that aren't yours because helping feels safer than holding boundaries. Meanwhile, your own work suffers and resentment builds.

These patterns aren't character flaws. They're survival strategies your Created Self developed to navigate environments where authenticity felt unsafe. The question is whether they're still serving you—or slowly draining you.

THE COST OF WORKPLACE PRETENDING

As you learned in Section 1, chasing approval leads to sacrificing your well-being. At work, this shows up as chronic stress, burnout, and the physical symptoms you explored earlier. Your body keeps score even when your mind insists you're fine.

Here's the deeper truth: You can't win by trying to meet others' expectations, because people interpret the same behavior completely differently.

I once worked late for two weeks because highway construction made rush hour traffic unbearable. I didn't want to sit in gridlock for hours, so I avoided it by staying late. One evening, a manager—not mine—saw me working and said hi. The next day, my manager told me this other manager was concerned about whether I could manage my workload. Why was I leaving late every day? What was preventing me from getting my work done in a reasonable amount of time?

The same behavior that some would praise as dedication, others judged as inefficiency. This is why authentic self-care at work isn't about pleasing everyone—it's about making conscious choices aligned with your actual needs rather than performing for approval that will always be inconsistent.

Beyond the physical cost, there's an emotional one. When you perform a version of yourself forty or more hours a week, you lose touch with who you actually are. Work becomes a place where your Authentic Self isn't welcome—and that grief accumulates quietly. Worse, the energy you spend performing at work is energy you can't use for your actual purpose—the relationships, creativity, service, or growth that matter most to you.

Recognizing these patterns is the first step. The next question is: how do you protect your Authentic Self while still earning a living? That's what the next article explores.

Intention of the Day
I will notice one Created Self pattern at work today so that I can choose differently.

Authentic Self-Care in the Workplace

You've recognized when your Created Self takes over at work. You've seen the cost—not just to your well-being, but to the energy you need for your actual purpose. Now comes the practical question: how do you protect yourself?

Authentic self-care in the workplace isn't about being unprofessional or ignoring legitimate responsibilities. It's about making conscious choices rather than automatic sacrifices. If your work IS your purpose, these strategies help you express it authentically rather than performing for approval. If your work funds your purpose, these strategies preserve the energy you need for what matters most.

PROTECTING YOUR AUTHENTIC SELF AT WORK

Know your limits before you cross them. As you learned in "Know Your Limits Before You Cross Them," understanding your actual capacity gives you power to set boundaries. This applies to workload, hours, and emotional labor. Notice when you're approaching your threshold and communicate it before you cross it.

USING PERMISSION TO SAY NO.

In "Permission to Say No," you explored how "no" protects your energy for what truly matters. At work, this might mean declining a project, pushing back on an unrealistic deadline, or refusing to be available around the clock.

After leaving graduate school, I worked in clinical research for several years. One week, my manager asked me on a Thursday morning to fly out and start a new assignment on Sunday. I told her no. She asked why. I explained that I had booked three separate healthcare appointments for that week—appointments scheduled months in advance—because it would be three months before I'd have another week without travel. She asked if I would reschedule. I said no. My health comes first.

I was firm on this boundary because for eight and a half years in graduate school, my health came last. That did not serve me well in the long run. The outcome of saying no? Nothing. I told her I wished I was in a position to help. She said okay. And that was that.

The consequences we fear often don't materialize. And even when they do, protecting your well-being is rarely the wrong choice.

Speak your truth when it matters. You explored this in "Speaking Your Truth." At work, this means contributing your perspective in meetings, advocating for yourself, and being honest about what you need. You can be professional and authentic at the same time.

Notice when you're performing. Use the signs you learned in "Signs You're Performing" to recognize when your Created Self has taken over at work. Physical tension, mental exhaustion, behavioral shifts—these signals apply in professional settings too. When you notice them, pause and reconnect with what's actually true for you.

FINDING WORKPLACES THAT HONOR YOUR AUTHENTIC SELF

Some work environments will never reward authenticity. If you've tried setting boundaries, speaking your truth, and protecting your well-being—and the workplace consistently punishes these choices—that's valuable information. Not every job deserves your Authentic Self. Some want only your labor.

When possible, seek workplaces and roles that align with your values. Notice during interviews whether the culture makes space for honesty, boundaries, and well-being. Trust your intuition when something feels off.

Whether your job is your purpose or funds it, you deserve a workplace that doesn't require you to abandon yourself. Your purpose—however you express it—deserves your energy. Don't let work steal all of it.

You spend too many hours at work to abandon yourself there. Your Authentic Self deserves to show up in every area of your life—including your career. The strategies in this article help you protect the energy and integrity you need for your actual purpose, whatever that may be.

Intention of the Day
I will set or hold one boundary at work today so that I honor my own needs.

Self-Care Tip: Know Your Priorities

You've identified your purpose and learned to protect it from workplace demands. As you learned in "Permission to Say No," protecting your time requires saying "no" to what doesn't serve you. But there's another threat to purpose-pursuit: filling your life with tasks that feel urgent but don't actually align with what matters most. One of the biggest obstacles to living your purpose is taking on tasks that don't serve it—including other people's priorities disguised as your own.

The Eisenhower Matrix helps you identify what deserves your time and what doesn't. This tool breaks tasks into four clear actions based on value, urgency, and who should handle them.

	Urgent	*Not Urgent*
Important	**Do it** (The Critical Zone) • Client presentation due tomorrow • Emergency that only you can resolve • Utility bill overdue	**Schedule it** (The Growth & Maintenance Zone) • Deep relationship time • Volunteer work • Annual tax filing
Not Important	**Delegate it** (The Support Zone) • Grocery shopping • Data entry • Lawn care	**Dump it/Say 'No'!** (The Distraction Zone) • Mindlessly scrolling social media • Reorganizing junk drawer • Deleting old emails • Perfecting presentation slides that no one will see

1. DO IT (THE CRITICAL ZONE)

High-stakes tasks that add significant value AND have looming deadlines (due today or tomorrow). Leaving these undone creates stress and negative consequences.

- *Work*: Client presentation due tomorrow morning
- *Home*: Utility bill due today to avoid disconnection

2. SCHEDULE IT (THE GROWTH & MAINTENANCE ZONE)

This category has two types. Always prioritize Value over Obligation when booking your time. Your Created Self will try to prioritize Obligation Tasks—they feel safer because someone expects them. Your Authentic Self knows that Value Tasks matter more because they serve your actual purpose, not just your perceived responsibilities. This is where living authentically requires conscious choice: schedule what matters to your Authentic Self before scheduling what others expect.

Value Tasks (High Priority): Add long-term value but aren't urgent. These are tasks that serve your actual purpose—the creative work, relationship time, skill-building, or service that your Authentic Self came here to do. Because they don't have external deadlines, they're easy to postpone indefinitely. That's why they get scheduled first.

- *Work (if purpose-aligned)*: Developing skills in your purpose area, strategic planning for meaningful projects, building relationships that support your purpose
- *Personal*: Creative practice, deep relationship time, volunteer work, spiritual practice, learning that feeds your purpose

Obligation Tasks (Lower Priority): Time-sensitive but don't add value—just maintenance requiring your expertise. Schedule these to get them "off your plate" without crowding out high-value work.

- *Work*: Mandatory administrative reports only you can complete
- *Home*: Filing annual taxes (requires your records but isn't growth)

3. DELEGATE IT (THE SUPPORT ZONE)

Time-sensitive tasks that don't require YOUR specific skill set. Delegating empowers others and frees you for tasks where your unique contribution matters most—including your actual purpose work. If you don't have a team at work, delegation might mean asking family to share household tasks, hiring help when possible, or using services (grocery delivery, meal kits) that buy back time for what matters.

- *Work*: Ask a colleague to format a document or enter data
- *Home*: Hire lawn service or ask family to pick up groceries

4. DUMP IT (THE DISTRACTION ZONE)

No value, not time-sensitive—pure distraction. These feel like "busy work" that creates the illusion of productivity.

- *Work*: Organizing old email folders with outdated information
- *Home*: Mindlessly scrolling social media, reorganizing junk drawers

Your Created Self may resist dumping tasks, insisting that responsible people handle everything. But time spent on low-value distractions is time stolen from your purpose. Dumping these tasks isn't lazy—it's protecting what matters.

KEY TAKEAWAY: PROTECT YOUR "VALUE" TIME

Most people fill their calendars with "Obligation" tasks because they feel urgent. To truly thrive, place your "Value" tasks on your calendar first, treating them as non-negotiable appointments with your future self.

When someone asks you to take on their task, run it through this matrix. If it's not in YOUR Critical Zone or Growth Zone, it belongs in Delegate or Dump. This isn't selfish—it's protecting your energy for your actual purpose. Your Authentic Self knows what deserves your time. This framework helps you honor that knowing.

When you're uncertain where a task belongs, use this decision tree to guide you:

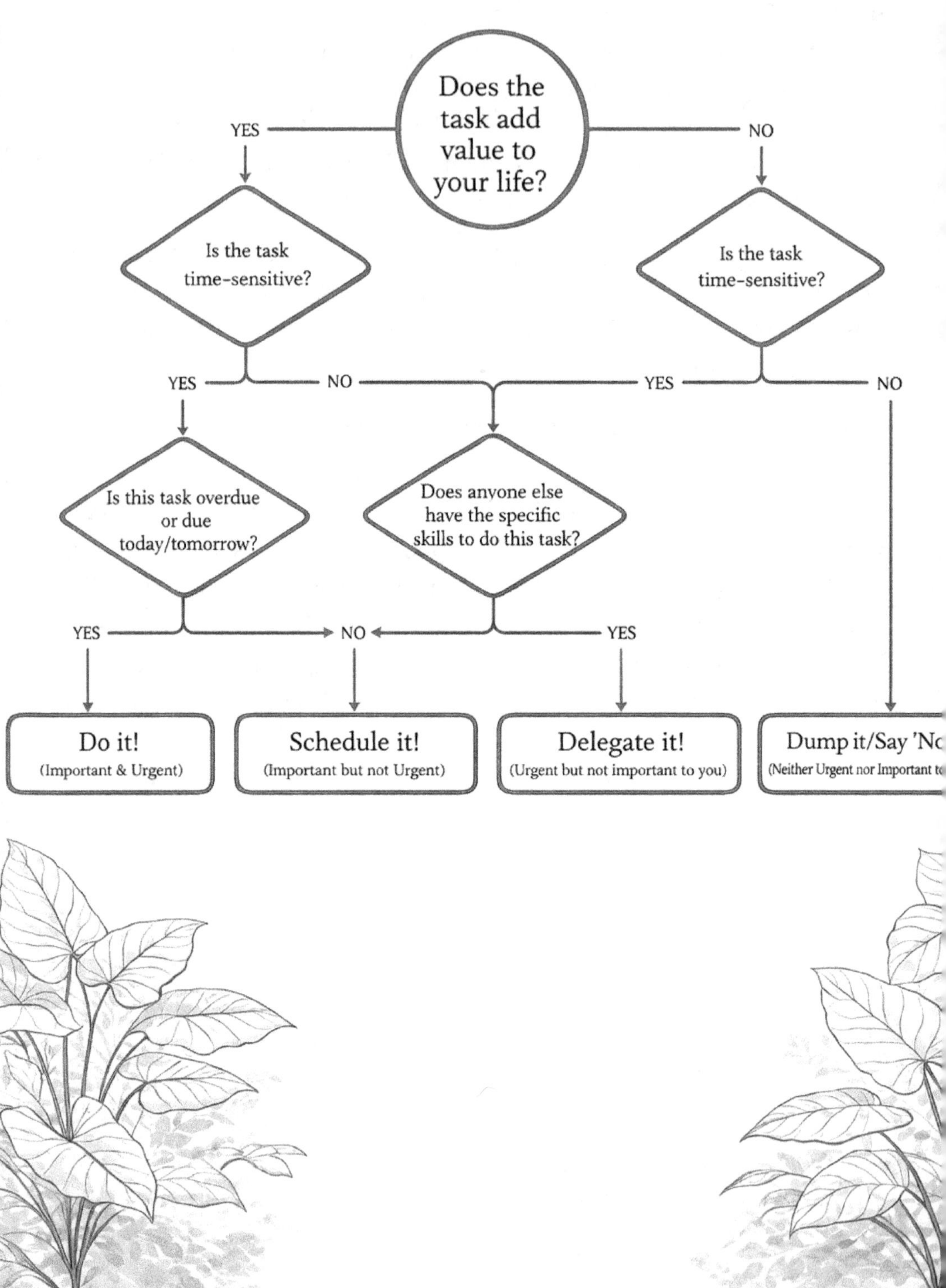

Does the task add value to your life?
YES
NO
Is the task time-sensitive?
Is the task time-sensitive?
YES
NO
YES
NO
Is this task overdue or due today/tomorrow?
Does anyone else have the specific skills to do this task?
YES
NO
YES
Do it!
(Important & Urgent)
Schedule it!
(Important but not Urgent)
Delegate it!
(Urgent but not important to you)
Dump it/Say 'No
(Neither Urgent nor Important to

Self-Care Tip: Make a Vision Board

You've identified what deserves your time and energy. Now comes a tool that keeps your purpose visible: the vision board. A vision board is a collection of images and words that represent your goals and desires—specifically, the purpose-aligned goals your Authentic Self is working toward.

Visualization works because your brain responds to images as if they were real experiences. When you regularly see pictures of your goals, your mind begins to recognize opportunities that align with them. You stay motivated because your vision remains in front of you rather than fading into the background of daily life. From an energy perspective, focusing on what you want attracts more of it into your life.

Here's the caution: vision boards can reinforce Created Self goals just as easily as Authentic Self purpose. If every image on your board serves external validation—impressing others, proving your worth, meeting someone else's definition of success—you're programming your brain toward exhaustion, not fulfillment. Before adding any image, ask: Is this what I actually want or what I think I should want?

Your Authentic Self doesn't care about impressing anyone. It cares about expressing who you truly are. The images you choose should make your soul say "yes, that's mine"—not "people will be impressed."

I create my vision boards digitally using Canva. I gather stock photos along with my own personal images, then assemble them into a single page. I print it out and place one copy in my daily planner and another on the wall above my computer. Seeing it every day keeps my goals alive in my mind.

My board includes images of me performing Reiki on a client, running up a flight of stairs with ease, a house of my own, three dogs, my business logo, the front cover of this book, a bank representing financial stability, the logo of the coaching company I work for, and a collection of crystals. Each image represents either my purpose—helping people care for their Authentic Self—or the health, home, companionship, and stability I need to sustain that purpose.

You can create a vision board with art supplies or digitally—whatever feels right to you. For a physical board, gather magazines, scissors, glue, and poster board. Cut out images and words that speak to you and arrange them however you like. For a digital version, use free tools like Canva or even a simple slideshow. Save it as your phone wallpaper or desktop background.

When choosing images, think beyond physical objects. Include pictures that represent how you want to feel. A woman smiling might reflect your desire for joy and peace. A person working calmly at a desk might represent focus and creative flow. Someone hiking alone might capture the freedom and presence you're seeking. These feeling-based images matter more than the objects because feelings reveal what your Authentic Self actually wants. Your Created Self chases things. Your Authentic Self seeks states of being.

Update your vision board every six months to a year. As you live more authentically, your Authentic Self reveals itself more fully. Dreams that once felt important may fall away because they were never truly yours. New visions emerge that you couldn't have imagined before. Your board should evolve as your Authentic Self becomes clearer.

Your vision board should be a mirror of your Authentic Self's purpose, not a catalog of your Created Self's achievements. When built authentically, this practice keeps your purpose visible, your motivation alive, and your brain actively seeking the opportunities that will help you live the life you're truly here to live.

Be Realistic

Your vision board shows where your purpose is leading you. Now comes the practical question: how do you get there without burning out along the way?

How often do you set goals for your purpose-work based on perfect conditions? You'll work on your purpose project every morning—if nothing unexpected happens. You'll launch your healing practice in three months—if no obstacles arise. You'll write that book in a year—if no emergencies come up. But life rarely offers perfect conditions. When your goals assume it will, you set yourself up for frustration and disappointment—not because your purpose is wrong, but because your timeline ignores reality.

Your vision board captures the destination. But getting there requires breaking that vision into achievable steps—steps that fit your actual life, not an imaginary one where nothing goes wrong.

This is your Created Self at work. It sets expectations based on who you think you should be rather than who you actually are. Your Created Self believes you should be able to do what everyone else appears to be doing—working full-time, raising kids, staying fit, and pursuing purpose without breaking a sweat. It compares your behind-the-scenes struggle to everyone else's highlight reel. It insists that needing more time or support means you're inadequate. Your Authentic Self knows something different: you can work only with the reality you actually have—your actual energy, your actual obligations, your actual capacity.

As you learned in "Know Your Limits Before You Cross Them," understanding your actual capacity helps you set boundaries. Here, that same self-knowledge helps you set realistic timelines. When you know your limits, you can plan within them—and actually meet your goals.

In my clinical research career, I learned to build in breathing room. When assigned a task I could complete in two weeks under ideal conditions, I'd commit to two and a half or three weeks instead. I knew things could go wrong—equipment malfunctions, delayed client responses, team members calling in sick, my own health needs. By planning for reality rather than perfection, I regularly delivered on time without sacrificing sleep, health, or quality. More importantly, I worried less. The breathing room protected both my work and my well-being.

A useful rule of thumb: whatever timeline feels comfortable, add 25-50% more time. If you think something will take four weeks, plan for five or six. This cushion accounts for the unexpected without feeling like you're moving too slowly.

The same principle applies to your purpose-work. If you want to start a coaching practice, don't tell yourself you'll have ten clients in three months—plan for five, and celebrate if you exceed that. If you're writing a book, don't commit to finishing in six months when you can write only on weekends—give yourself a year. If you're building a creative practice, don't promise daily sessions when three times a week is actually sustainable. Realistic goals keep you moving forward. Unrealistic ones make you quit.

Your Created Self may protest that realistic goals mean settling for less, that you're not trying hard enough, that you should push yourself harder. But pushing yourself into burnout doesn't serve your purpose—it kills it. Sustainable progress always beats unsustainable intensity.

Start where you actually are, not where you think you should be.

Realistic goals reduce worry and build confidence. Each one you meet reinforces that you can trust yourself—and that trust is essential for pursuing your purpose long-term. Your Authentic Self knows this journey is a marathon, not a sprint. Setting goals that honor your actual capacity isn't lowering your standards. It's respecting the reality that sustainable purpose-work requires sustainable pacing.

Intention of the Day
I will set goals that honor my reality so I can meet them with confidence.

Self-Care Tip: Budget for Peace of Mind

Realistic timelines protect your energy for purpose-work. But there's another resource that either enables or blocks purpose: money.

You've identified your purpose and planned realistic steps toward it. But here's a practical obstacle many people face: money anxiety that drains the mental and emotional energy purpose-work requires. Financial health is part of whole health. When money feels chaotic, that stress spills into every other area of your life—your sleep, your relationships, your ability to focus. Most importantly, financial chaos makes it nearly impossible to pursue your purpose. You can't create, serve, or grow when you're constantly worried about making rent. Budgeting isn't just about numbers—it's about creating the financial foundation your purpose needs.

When you don't budget, you rely on your brain to remember every bill, every due date, every amount. But your mind already has enough to manage. Without a written plan, it's easy to overpay one bill, underpay another, or forget one entirely. Then come the overdraft fees, the scramble to borrow from friends, the shame spiral. Not budgeting creates more chaos—and more work—than budgeting ever does.

I know this from experience. When I skip budgeting, things fall apart. I've had overdraft fees. I've had to ask friends for emergency loans. Each time, I'm reminded that the effort of budgeting saves me from far greater effort later. When I do budget, I feel calmer and more confident around money. The chaos quiets.

This is your Authentic Self in action—facing reality clearly rather than avoiding it. Your Created Self wants to pretend money isn't a problem or believes you should magically be better at finances without actually tracking anything. Your Authentic Self knows that awareness creates choice. When you see where money actually goes, you can redirect it toward what serves your purpose rather than what drains it.

A budget also helps you align your spending with your values. When you see where your money goes, you can ask deeper questions. Are you paying rent just to satisfy another bill, or are you investing in your personal sanctuary? Are you buying clothes to impress others, or to feel comfortable and confident? Are you spending on subscriptions you don't use because canceling feels like too much effort? This clarity reduces stress because your money starts working for your actual life—and your actual purpose—not someone else's expectations.

GETTING STARTED

You don't need anything fancy to begin. A pen and paper work fine. So does a simple spreadsheet. Apps like Credit Karma or YNAB can automate tracking if you prefer digital tools. What matters is finding a method you'll actually use.

Start by listing your income and fixed expenses—rent, utilities, subscriptions. Then track your variable spending for one month to see where money actually goes. From there, you can adjust. The goal isn't perfection. It's awareness. Most smartphones have built-in screen time tracking. Use similar thinking for money: awareness motivates change without judgment.

If you've tried to budget but find yourself repeatedly avoiding it, a financial therapist can help. They address the emotional and psychological barriers to managing money—not just the practical steps. Sometimes the block isn't about math. It's about what money represents. The next article explores this deeper relationship with money and the beliefs that shape how you earn, spend, and save.

IF YOU'RE PURSUING PURPOSE THROUGH SELF-EMPLOYMENT

If you're building purpose through self-employment or a side business, one critical practice: keep separate budgets for business and personal finances. When the two get muddled, everything becomes harder to track—and tax season becomes a nightmare. Separate budgets create clarity and save you hours of untangling later. I'm learning this lesson myself right now. When business and personal finances blur together, confusion follows.

Budgeting takes effort, but it returns peace of mind—and mental energy. When money stops being a constant worry, that energy becomes available for your actual purpose. Financial clarity isn't just about paying bills on time. It's about freeing yourself to pursue what you're here to do.

Money Beliefs That Block Your Purpose

You receive an unexpected windfall—a tax refund, a bonus, a gift. For a moment, you feel relief. Maybe even hope. Then, within weeks, something happens. The car breaks down. A medical bill arrives. An appliance dies. The money vanishes as quickly as it came.

If this pattern sounds familiar, you're not imagining it. And it's not bad luck. It's a money belief in action.

In "Self-Care Tip: Budget for Peace of Mind," you explored practical tools for managing money. But financial self-care goes deeper than spreadsheets and tracking expenses. It includes your emotional relationship with money—the beliefs, fears, and patterns that shape how you earn, spend, save, and give.

These patterns don't affect just your bank account. They affect whether you can actually pursue your purpose. If inherited beliefs tell you that money always disappears, you won't trust abundance when it arrives. If trauma makes you distrust help, you won't hire support that could free your time. If guilt says spending on yourself is selfish, you won't invest in the training or tools your purpose needs.

Your relationship with money either enables or blocks your purpose. Understanding that relationship is essential.

INHERITED BELIEFS ABOUT MONEY

Think about the messages you absorbed growing up. Did your family talk about money with fear or shame? Did you witness financial struggle despite hard work? Did you learn that money is scarce, unreliable, or dangerous?

I inherited the belief that money will eventually disappear. I watched family members struggle with financial security no matter how hard they worked. This created a quiet expectation that any money coming to me wouldn't last. And for years, that belief seemed to confirm itself. Whenever I received a windfall—tax returns, multiple sign-ups for my business events—something would immediately require I spend it. Unexpected car repairs. Medical bills. The money vanished as quickly as it arrived.

This belief makes it hard to invest in my purpose. When an opportunity arises—a training program, a marketing investment, equipment I need—my first thought is "this money won't last anyway." That hesitation has cost me growth opportunities my purpose needed.

Your Created Self absorbed these beliefs without questioning them. It treats them as facts rather than interpretations. Your Authentic Self can examine them and ask: Is this actually true? Does believing this serve my well-being and purpose? Or does it keep me trapped in patterns that don't fit who I actually am?

TRUST AND MONEY

Your experiences shape how much you trust others around money. For me, that trust was damaged early. People stole money and supplies from my father's business. As a child, I caught a housekeeper trying to steal from my piggy bank. These experiences taught me that others couldn't be trusted with my finances—a reasonable conclusion for a child trying to make sense of betrayal.

But that childhood learning became an adult limitation. Now, hiring accountants, tax preparers, and lawyers—professionals who could ease my financial burden—feels risky. The vulnerability of letting someone else see my numbers or manage my money triggers old protective patterns. I'm learning to distinguish between the real child who needed those walls and the adult who needs help she can afford to get.

Your Created Self built walls to protect you. Those walls made sense when you were vulnerable. But now they may prevent you from receiving help you need. Your Authentic Self knows the difference between reasonable caution and self-imposed isolation. Not everyone will betray you—and refusing all help guarantees you'll struggle alone.

This distrust affects my purpose-work directly. I struggle to hire the designers and support staff who could free my time for what only I can do. The risk of letting someone else into my business triggers old protection patterns—even when the risk is minimal and the benefit is clear.

Giving and Worth

When I worked in clinical research and earned a comfortable salary, I bought gifts freely and donated to charities. Generosity felt natural because resources were abundant. When I left that career and my income dropped, giving became painful. I couldn't care for others the way I once did. Guilt crept in—as if my worth depended on what I could provide financially.

This revealed a Created Self belief: that my value to others required money. Learning to give in other ways—time, attention, skill, presence— has been humbling and healing. Your concern for others doesn't require a budget line. Love isn't transactional, even when your Created Self insists it is.

Guilt Around Spending on Yourself

Even when you understand that self-care matters, spending money on yourself can trigger guilt—especially when debt exists. Your Created Self may insist that every dollar should go toward obligation, not nourishment. That caring for yourself is wasteful when bills remain unpaid.

I've felt this guilt. Spending on massage, supplements, or coaching felt irresponsible when credit card balances loomed. But I've learned that self-care isn't wasteful—it's foundational. You can honor financial obligations and invest in your well-being. Both matter. Depleting yourself to pay down debt faster doesn't serve your whole health—or your purpose.

This guilt becomes especially problematic when your purpose requires investment. Training programs, professional development, business expenses, creative supplies—pursuing your purpose often costs money. If guilt blocks every self-investment, you'll stay stuck in work that pays the bills but starves your soul.

Your Created Self insists that every dollar should go toward obligation, not growth. Your Authentic Self knows differently: strategic investment in yourself and your purpose isn't selfish. It's how you build the capacity to serve others more fully.

Working With Your Money Beliefs

Recognizing limiting beliefs is the first step. But awareness alone doesn't shift patterns that have been running for decades. You need practices that help you build a new relationship with money—one grounded in your Authentic Self rather than inherited fears.

Financial therapist Bari Tessler, author of *The Art of Money*, offers a framework for this deeper work. Her approach combines practical money skills with emotional and body-based awareness. Here are practices adapted from her methodology:

Start with your body. Before opening a bank statement, paying bills, or making a financial decision, pause and notice what's happening physically. Is your chest tight? Is your breathing shallow? Are your shoulders creeping toward your ears? Money triggers survival responses. Checking in with your body interrupts the autopilot reaction and creates space for conscious choice.

Trace the belief back. When you notice a money pattern—like my "windfall disappears" belief—ask yourself: Where did I learn this? Who taught me this, directly or indirectly? Understanding the origin helps you see the belief as inherited rather than inevitable. You didn't choose it. You can examine it.

Schedule regular "money dates." Tessler recommends setting aside dedicated time—weekly or monthly—to engage with your finances without crisis driving the interaction. Light a candle. Make tea. Approach your numbers with curiosity rather than dread. This practice transforms money from an emergency you avoid into a relationship you tend.

Create micro counter-experiences. Beliefs shift through experience, not just insight. If you believe money always disappears, experiment with setting aside a small amount—even five dollars—that you protect fiercely. Watch it stay. If you believe you can't trust others with money, hire someone for a tiny task and notice what happens. Small experiments build new evidence.

Separate shame from information. A low bank balance is information. It tells you something about your current situation. It says nothing about your worth, your intelligence, or your future. When shame floods in, name it: "This is shame. It's not information." Then return to the numbers with as much neutrality as you can access.

EXAMINING YOUR MONEY BELIEFS

Take a moment to reflect:

- What did you learn about money growing up?
- What emotions arise when you think about your finances—fear, shame, anxiety, guilt?
- Where do you notice scarcity thinking—the belief that there's never enough?
- Where might abundance thinking serve you better—trusting that what you need will come?

Now connect these beliefs to your purpose:

- Do your money beliefs make it easier or harder to pursue your purpose?
- If you believed you were worthy of financial stability, how would that change your choices?
- What purpose-supporting investment (training, tools, help) have you avoided because of money fear or guilt?
- If money anxiety disappeared tomorrow, what would you do differently?

These aren't questions to answer once and forget. Your relationship with money evolves as you do. Financial self-care means returning to these questions periodically, with curiosity rather than judgment.

Use the same process you learned in "Questioning Beliefs That No Longer Serve You": Notice the belief. Ask if it's true. Ask if it helps. If it doesn't serve your purpose, you have permission to release it.

MOVING FORWARD

You don't have to heal every money belief today. Start by noticing. When money anxiety or guilt arises this week, pause and ask: What belief is driving this feeling? Is it actually true? Does it serve my purpose, or does it block it?

If money patterns feel deeply stuck, consider working with a financial therapist. As mentioned earlier, they help address the emotional barriers that budgeting alone can't fix. Some money wounds need professional support to heal.

Your Authentic Self knows that financial well-being includes peace of mind, not just balanced accounts. Money is a tool for living—not a measure of your worth. Caring for your financial health means caring for your beliefs about money, not just the numbers themselves.

Intention of the Day

I will notice one belief about money today and ask whether it serves my purpose or blocks it.

Worry Reveals Opportunity

In October 2025, Hurricane Melissa struck Jamaica as the strongest recorded hurricane in Atlantic history. I was livid and terrified. I worried for my family and for the people of Jamaica in general. There was so much devastation in the country, and I felt hopeless about being able to do anything about it living here in the United States.

PROCESSING BEFORE ACTING

In those first days, before I could do anything practical, I needed to process what I was feeling. So I wrote a letter—not to a person, but to Jamaica itself.

I thanked my country for its resilience, for protecting my family through generations of storms, for the strength that lives in its hills and in the blood of its people scattered across the world. I wrote about how Jamaicans handled Hurricane Gilbert when I was a child—how most other countries could never have borne what we went through. I acknowledged that my heart was heavy, that I knew my country was about to be tested at a level we hadn't seen. And I wrote this:

"My body and blood, as well as that of thousands upon thousands of people all across the world, come directly from you and remain spiritually linked and indebted to you. No matter how far away I am from you, I still take you with me wherever I go. To be so powerful from afar means you cannot be defeated."

Writing that letter didn't fix anything. The hurricane was still coming. My family was still in danger. But something shifted in me. The helplessness loosened its grip. I could feel my connection to something larger than my fear—to my ancestors, to my culture, to the resilience that runs through Jamaican blood. From that grounded place, I was able to take the next step.

FROM PROCESSING TO ACTION

After a few days, I knew I had to do something practical. So I started an Amazon wishlist for hurricane disaster relief supplies that I could take down to Jamaica for Thanksgiving—a trip I'd already planned. I sent out the wishlist to all my friends, family, coworkers, and on social media. I also sent it to my Reiki clients and students.

The wishlist was fulfilled in less than 48 hours.

That moment showed me something I hadn't been fully aware of: my tribe was much bigger than I realized. People I barely knew contributed. Colleagues I'd only worked with briefly stepped up. Students from one Reiki class mobilized their own networks. The speed and generosity revealed a community I hadn't been consciously tending—but who showed up the moment there was a clear way to help.

I was able to take down three checked suitcases of supplies to Jamaica. Many people who saw the wishlist was already fulfilled decided to donate money instead, so I took that money to Jamaica and purchased food and water locally. My mother, my brother, my mother's friend, and I drove into the disaster area and distributed supplies to the community my mother's family was from.

I felt so much better afterward—not just relief, but genuine purpose fulfillment. I had been able to convert that worry for my country into compassionate action. And I had discovered the reach of my tribe in the process.

WORRY AS ENERGY

Here's what that experience taught me: worry itself solves nothing. But the energy behind it can be redirected—sometimes through spiritual practice, sometimes through practical action, often through both.

The letter I wrote was a form of redirection. Instead of letting fear spiral into paralysis, I channeled it into gratitude and connection. That spiritual processing didn't replace action—it enabled it. I needed to ground myself before I could think clearly about what to do.

When I moved to Connecticut for college, the first winter was freezing cold. I wanted to buy wool clothing, but it was too expensive. Naturally, I worried about how I would handle the next winter. However, later that summer, I had two weeks free before classes started. Because I was bored and still anxious about the cold, I decided to take action. I bought yarn, knitting needles, and a book to learn the skill. I knitted a hat and scarf that first summer. In the twenty-five years since, I've made hats, scarves, socks, gloves, and sweaters. I knit gifts for family and friends, which saves money. I also knit hats to donate to charity.

But knitting became more than a solution to cold winters. It became part of how I express care—every gift I knit carries my attention and love. It became a way to serve others through charity donations. It taught me that I'm capable of learning hard things when I commit to the process. And it showed me that limitations (not enough money for wool clothing) can become doorways to discovery. That worried college student had no idea she was starting a 25-year practice that would feed her soul.

PRODUCTIVE CONCERN VS. USELESS WORRY

Your Created Self believes worry serves you. It insists that if you worry enough, you'll somehow prevent bad outcomes or prove you care. But worry without action—or without intentional processing—is just mental spinning. It exhausts you without moving you forward.

Your Authentic Self knows the difference between productive concern and useless worry.

Productive concern asks: "What can I do about this?" and moves toward action. It might also ask: "What do I need to process before I can act?" It surveys the situation, identifies options, and takes a step—even a small one. Productive concern respects the problem without being consumed by it.

Useless worry asks: "What if everything goes wrong?" and spirals into disaster scenarios that may never happen. It replays the same fears without generating solutions or releasing the emotional weight. It drains your energy while the situation remains unchanged.

The spiritual teacher Eckhart Tolle said, "Worry pretends to be necessary but serves no useful purpose." The problem stays difficult whether you worry or not. The goal stays the same. Staying peaceful during a challenge saves energy—but that's easier said than done.

The key is learning to redirect worry-energy quickly, before it spirals. Sometimes that redirection is practical action. Sometimes it's emotional or spiritual processing. Both count.

HOW TO REDIRECT WORRY INTO ACTION

When you notice worry arising, use this process:

Step 1: Name it. Acknowledge what you're worried about. Say it clearly to yourself: "I'm worried about my family in Jamaica." "I'm worried about affording winter clothes." "I'm worried about this deadline at work." Naming the worry externalizes it—you're observing the worry rather than drowning in it.

Step 2: Ask what you need first. Sometimes you can act immediately. Other times, you need to process the emotion before you can think clearly. Ask yourself: "Do I need to ground myself before I can take action?" If so, write, pray, meditate, talk to someone you trust, or use one of the grounding techniques from "Self-Care Tip: Ground & Center." This isn't avoiding action—it's preparing for it.

Step 3: Ask one action question. "What's one action I can take right now?" Not the perfect action. Not the complete solution. Just one thing you can do today—or in the next hour—that moves you from helpless to engaged.

Step 4: Take that action. Start the wishlist. Buy the yarn. Send the email. Make the phone call. The action doesn't have to be big. It has to be real. Movement interrupts the spiral.

Step 5: Repeat as needed. After one action, you may feel relief—or you may still feel worried. If worry returns, repeat the process. Ask again: "What's one more action I can take?" Each small step builds momentum and reduces the grip of helpless fear.

This process works because it honors both the emotional and practical dimensions of worry. You're not suppressing the concern or pretending everything is fine. You're responding to the worry with presence and purpose.

WHEN WORRY REVEALS LARGER POSSIBILITIES

Sometimes redirecting worry doesn't just solve the immediate problem—it opens doors you never expected.

My worry about Jamaica led me to discover the true reach of my tribe. My letter to Jamaica reconnected me with ancestral strength I'd forgotten I could access. My worry about cold winters led me to a 25-year practice of creative expression and generosity. In each case, the worry itself was the doorway. What felt like a problem became an opportunity for growth, connection, and purpose.

As you work through your own worries, stay open to this possibility. The skill you develop, the people you connect with, the spiritual resources you discover, the strength you build—these may serve you far beyond the original concern. Worry can be a gateway to discovering capabilities and communities you didn't know you had.

WHEN WORRY BECOMES OVERWHELMING

Some people stay calm during hard times. They've learned to redirect worry-energy quickly rather than letting it spiral. This isn't a special gift—it's a skill you can develop through practice.

But if worry becomes overwhelming—keeping you up at night, interfering with daily functioning, or creating physical symptoms—that's when to seek professional support. As you learned in "Self-Care Tip: When to Seek Professional Help" in Section 4, recognizing when you need more than self-help strategies is wisdom, not weakness. Anxiety disorders are real, and they respond to treatment. Transforming worry into opportunity works for typical life concerns. Persistent, debilitating worry needs clinical support.

Whichever path you take, the principle remains: don't let worry sit idle. Give it somewhere useful to go—whether that's a letter, a prayer, a practical step, or a conversation with someone who can help.

Intention of the Day
I will notice one worry today and ask: What action can I take that serves my purpose?

Failure is Normal

I hate to break it to you, but our lives are built on failure. You wouldn't have known how to walk without first falling on your diapered baby bum a few times. So, if failure is required to learn the basic human function of walking, why is it considered a bad thing?

This matters especially when you're pursuing your purpose. The work that calls to your soul often requires you to try things you've never done before, enter spaces where you're not the expert, and risk falling on your face. Your Created Self sees this risk and screams "Don't try! You'll fail!" Your Authentic Self knows the truth: failure is how you find your way to what you're here to do.

Failure is how we learn what works and what doesn't.

WHEN FAILURE FINDS YOU

Your Created Self is terrified of failure. It learned early that mistakes led to criticism, shame, or disappointment from others. So it keeps you playing small, choosing only what you're already good at, staying in situations that feel safe even when they're slowly draining you. It would rather have you miserable in a "successful" life than risk failing at something that actually matters to you.

But sometimes failure finds you whether you're ready or not.

I experienced this firsthand. I was working in clinical research, performing well, when my manager submitted me for a promotion. About a month later, the promotions were announced. My colleagues were promoted. I wasn't—even though I was a top performer in my department.

Something felt wrong, but I didn't know what. My manager was out of town for a client meeting and didn't yet know my promotion hadn't gone through. I couldn't ask her what happened. Then a coworker who'd been at the company for five years told me that whenever mass layoffs occurred, they always happened around that time of year.

Something told me to start applying for jobs. So I did. I updated my CV and LinkedIn profile. I applied to seven positions. Three days later, I was laid off—along with twelve percent of the company.

WORKING THROUGH FAILURE FEELINGS

Because I'd listened to my intuition, I was mentally prepared for the possibility. But that didn't erase the emotional weight.

I worried intensely about how my family in Jamaica would see it. In Jamaican culture, there's no distinction between being fired and being laid off. In their minds, if I wasn't a failure, the company would have chosen someone else to let go. I was so anxious about their reaction that I didn't tell them for a month. They found out by accident—I was getting my mail in the middle of the day while on the phone with my mother, and she asked why I was home.

What helped me process the shame and fear was treating the job search as my new full-time job. I searched online every day—Indeed, Glassdoor, individual company websites. I attended every clinical research job fair I could find. I networked at every Toastmasters meeting within a twenty-mile radius. I did informational interviews with people in the industry.

Action became my way through. I couldn't control how my family perceived me. I couldn't undo the layoff. But I could show up every day and take the next step. That structure kept me from spiraling into shame.

I also let myself feel sad—not for myself, but for my coworkers. I saw some of them crying as they packed up their desks. It was heartbreaking. Allowing that sadness was part of processing the experience honestly, rather than rushing past it.

When Failure Redirects You

Six weeks after the layoff, everything changed.

I interviewed for a contract position that paid less than my previous job. The interview apparently went well, because as I was leaving, reception stopped me and sent me back to the interview room. They told me they thought I'd be better suited for a different position they had open.

That position paid forty percent more than the job I'd lost.

They interviewed me for it that same day. By the time I got home, they called to offer me the job. It was a Friday, and they wanted me to start Tuesday.

What others might have judged as failure became redirection toward something better. Whether my family saw it as failure or not didn't change the outcome—it still led me exactly where I needed to go. And that stepping stone eventually led to another, and another, until I found my way to the work I do now.

Failure Doesn't Define You

Oprah Winfrey was fired from her first television job as an anchor in Baltimore. They told her she was "unfit for television news"—too emotional, too empathetic, not detached enough. That "failure" forced her to question whether traditional news was actually her path. It wasn't. Morning talk shows welcomed the very qualities news rejected: her emotional intelligence, her ability to connect, her genuine curiosity about people's stories. That firing didn't end her television career. It redirected her toward the work she was actually meant to do—creating conversations that changed millions of lives.

Thomas Edison famously failed around twelve hundred times before creating a working light bulb. But here's what matters: each failure taught him something. This material doesn't work. That design creates too much heat. This filament burns out too quickly. He wasn't failing randomly—he was systematically eliminating what wouldn't work, getting closer to what would.

These examples aren't just about persistence. They're about people who discovered their true purpose through failure. Oprah's firing revealed she wasn't meant for traditional journalism. Edison's failures taught him what wouldn't work, clearing the path to what would. Failure doesn't block your purpose. It reveals it.

GETTING BACK UP

When you face a setback, these practices help you move forward:

Allow the disappointment first. Don't rush to extract lessons or silver linings. Let yourself feel the loss, the frustration, the sadness. Emotions that get pushed aside don't disappear—they resurface later. Give yourself a day, a week, whatever you need. Then shift to action.

Separate the failure from your identity. You experienced a failure. You are not a failure. Your Created Self wants to collapse these into one thing. Your Authentic Self knows the difference. What happened is an event. Who you are remains intact.

Let action be your path through. When shame or fear threatens to paralyze you, movement helps. It doesn't have to be the perfect next step—just a step. Apply for one job. Make one phone call. Take one class. Action interrupts the spiral and rebuilds your sense of agency.

Ask what this failure is teaching you. Once you've processed the emotions, get curious. What does success look like now? Why didn't this work? What haven't I tried? Who can help? What is this failure revealing about my actual purpose? Maybe it's showing you what doesn't fit so you can move toward what does.

YOU'VE DONE THIS BEFORE

Fear of failure is one of the biggest obstacles to living your purpose. You know there's something you're called to do—a business you want to start, a creative project that pulls at you, a career change that would align with your values. But what if you try and fail?

Remember this: you've already survived failures. Every one of them eventually led somewhere. The baby who kept falling learned to walk. The fired news anchor became Oprah. The researcher who failed twelve hundred times lit up the world. The laid-off employee found work that paid more and meant more.

Failure isn't the opposite of success. It's how you find your way there.

Intention of the Day
I will treat every failure as a stepping stone to success.

What Imperfection Teaches You

Failure teaches you what doesn't work. Imperfection teaches you what you actually need—even when something is working well enough.

There is no circumstance in life that is perfect. Whether it is your career, relationships, home, body, or skills, nothing will ever be fully favorable. Your Created Self may resist this truth, always seeking an ideal that doesn't exist.

This resistance keeps many people from pursuing their purpose. They wait for perfect circumstances—enough money saved, the right credentials, ideal timing, full family support. But perfect circumstances never arrive. Your purpose isn't waiting for perfection. It's waiting for you to start where you are, with what you have, learning as you go.

But your Authentic Self knows something important: flaws provide chances for growth and discovery.

Your Created Self was taught that if you work hard enough, plan carefully enough, and do everything "right," you'll achieve the perfect career, relationship, or life. When reality falls short, your Created Self sees failure. Your Authentic Self sees information. It asks: What is this imperfection teaching me? What does this reveal about what I actually need versus what I thought I should want?

Imperfection is a teacher. Each situation that falls short of ideal reveals something about what you actually need.

This matters especially when you're discovering your purpose. You might try work you think should fulfill you—but the imperfect reality reveals it doesn't. You might pursue a path that looks right from the outside—but the struggles show you it's not aligned with your Authentic Self. These aren't wasted experiences. They're essential data showing you what your purpose actually requires.

I learned this through my career. One job had a heavy workload with an understaffed team—we were stretched thin constantly. But I enjoyed it because everyone was reliable, our workflows were efficient, and we communicated well. The workload didn't drain me when the team functioned smoothly.

Other jobs paid high salaries, which looked perfect on paper. But I was rarely home, exhausted all the time, and never felt I was contributing anything meaningful to society. The money didn't compensate for feeling disconnected from purpose.

I worked on a project that was chaotic, missed deadlines constantly, and lacked basic resources we needed to succeed. It should have been miserable. But I enjoyed solving the problems, helped people in genuine need, and the client was pleased despite the chaos. The dysfunction didn't matter as much when the work itself was meaningful.

My Created Self saw three imperfect jobs and felt frustrated by each one. My Authentic Self gathered essential information: what energizes me (problem-solving, helping people in need) and what depletes me (meaningless work, no time at home) matters more than what looks good externally (high salary, impressive title).

What did I learn from all of that? My ideal job involves solving problems, has great team communication, allows quality time at home, and helps people in need—even with a heavy workload and changing schedule. No single job was perfect. But together, they taught me what I truly value. Those imperfect experiences led me toward the work I do now—work that actually aligns with my purpose.

This principle extends beyond career. Maybe you volunteer with an organization whose mission you support, but the disorganization frustrates you. That imperfection teaches you that efficiency matters to you—information that helps you choose future volunteer work or even identify skills you could offer (helping organizations improve their systems). Maybe you try a creative practice that doesn't come naturally. The struggle reveals whether the challenge energizes you (sign you're on the right path) or depletes you (sign this particular expression isn't your purpose). Imperfect experiences aren't obstacles to discovering your purpose. They're how you discover it.

This doesn't mean tolerating situations that harm you. There's a difference between imperfection that teaches and toxicity that depletes. As you learned in "Boundaries as Healing" in Section 4, recognizing when to walk away protects your well-being. Imperfection that reveals your values serves you. Imperfection that violates your boundaries doesn't. Your Authentic Self knows the difference.

With each struggle and obstacle comes a chance to learn what you need to feel fulfilled, what you cannot bear, and what costs you little in the pursuit of happiness. Imperfection isn't blocking your path. It's lighting the way toward your purpose.

Your purpose isn't hiding in perfect circumstances. It's revealed through imperfect ones—the struggles that show you what you care about, the limitations that force creative solutions, the failures that redirect you toward what actually fits. Each imperfect situation is an invitation to learn what your Authentic Self needs to thrive.

As you learned in "Questioning Beliefs That No Longer Serve You," you can release the belief that perfect circumstances are required before you pursue what matters. And as "Failure is Normal" showed you, setbacks aren't endings—they're information. Imperfection works the same way. It's not a sign you're on the wrong path. It's guidance showing you what your path actually needs.

It's not about finding grass that's greener—chasing an ideal that doesn't exist. It's about finding grass you're least allergic to—work and life that align with your actual values and needs, even when they're imperfect.

Intention of the Day
I will notice what imperfect situations teach me about what I truly need.

Worth the Wait

You're two years into building something that matters to you. Maybe it's a business, a creative project, a career transition, or a skill you're developing. You've done the work. You've shown up consistently. But results are slow, and lately doubt has crept in. Is this actually going anywhere? Am I wasting my time? Maybe I should just quit.

This is the hardest part of pursuing your purpose: the middle. The beginning has excitement. The end has celebration. But the middle? The middle is where most people give up.

THE SIMMERING PHASE

Whenever I decide to make gumbo, Bolognese meat sauce, or braised oxtails, it's after I build myself up physically and mentally for the process. I remind myself that the results are worth the effort.

Building myself up means thinking through everything the process requires and committing to it completely. Setting aside time to purchase the ingredients. Cleaning and seasoning the meat. Chopping the vegetables. Combining everything in the right order to bring out the best flavors. Letting it all simmer for one and a half to two hours. I take a deep breath and get started.

As the pot simmers, the aroma wafts throughout my home, signaling that the fruit of my labor is almost ready. But I still have to clean up the kitchen, wash dishes, and take out the trash. Then, when the food is finally cooked and I take my first bite, I'm reminded it was all worth it.

The process is the same for pursuing your purpose—the work that makes your heart sing.

Building yourself up means acknowledging this will require real effort and committing anyway. Setting aside time means protecting space for purpose-work, even when other demands compete. Purchasing ingredients means gathering the resources, skills, and support you need. Cleaning and seasoning means preparing yourself mentally and emotionally. Chopping vegetables means breaking big dreams into actionable steps. Combining everything in the right order means following a process that makes sense, even when results aren't visible yet.

And the simmering—that one-and-a-half to two-hour wait while transformation happens invisibly—that's the hardest part. You're doing the work but can't see results yet. Doubt whispers that nothing is happening. You wonder if the effort will pay off. Your Created Self wants to abandon the pot, order takeout, declare the whole thing a waste. Your Authentic Self knows: this is when the magic happens. Stay with the process.

THREE YEARS OF SIMMERING

I've been writing this book for over three years. There have been moments when I wondered if it would ever be finished. Moments when other obligations pulled my attention away. Moments when I questioned whether anyone would actually read it.

What keeps me going is my daily work with clients and students.

When a health coaching client shares a struggle with burnout, and I offer a perspective that helps them see their situation differently, I'm reminded that the same perspective is in this book. When a Reiki student asks how to handle feeling drained by other people's energy and I teach them a grounding technique that changes their experience, I'm reminded that technique is in this book too.

Every conversation validates that this book has a purpose and an audience. The people I help remind me daily that others are waiting for these same tools—people I'll never meet, people who will find this book when they need it most.

That's what sustains me through the simmering. Not blind faith that it will work out, but evidence from my daily life that the content matters.

THE PSYCHOLOGY OF PATIENCE

Research on what psychologists call "grit" shows that passion and perseverance for long-term goals predict success better than talent alone. Angela Duckworth's studies found that the ability to sustain effort over years—not months—distinguishes those who achieve meaningful goals from those who don't.

But grit isn't about forcing yourself through misery by sheer willpower. It's about maintaining connection to why your goal matters while accepting that the timeline isn't fully in your control.

Other research shows the value of "process focus" over "outcome focus." When you fixate on the end result—publication, profit, recognition—every day without that result feels like failure. When you focus on the process—did I do today's work?—every day you show up is a success. The outcome eventually follows the process, but only if you stay with the process long enough.

STAYING COMMITTED WHEN DOUBT CREEPS IN

Here are practices that help when the middle feels endless:

Reconnect with your why. When doubt whispers that you're wasting time, return to the reason you started. Not the external rewards you hope for, but the deeper purpose underneath. Write it down. Say it out loud. Let it anchor you.

Find evidence in your daily life. Like my work with clients reminds me this book has an audience, look for moments that validate your purpose. When someone benefits from somrthing you're building, notice it. Let those moments be fuel.

Measure process, not just outcomes. Create metrics you can control. Did you show up today? Did you complete the task you planned? Those are wins, regardless of whether the big goal is visible yet.

Celebrate small completions. The journey toward a large goal contains many smaller completions. A chapter drafted. A skill learned. A connection made. Each one deserves acknowledgment—not because you need constant praise, but because recognition sustains momentum.

Expect doubt and plan for it. Doubt isn't a sign you're on the wrong path—it's a normal part of any meaningful pursuit. When it arrives, don't treat it as evidence that you should quit. Treat it as a familiar visitor that comes and goes. Acknowledge it, then return to the work.

WHEN PATIENCE RUNS OUT

Sometimes what feels like impatience is actually important information.

If you've been pursuing something for years and feel no connection to it anymore—if the work itself brings no satisfaction, only the hoped-for outcome—that's worth examining. As you learned in "What Imperfection Teaches You," struggles reveal what you actually need. Persistent emptiness might indicate this particular path isn't yours, even if the broader purpose is.

But if the work itself still matters to you—if showing up still feels meaningful even when progress is slow—that's your Authentic Self telling you to stay. The timeline isn't the point. The purpose is.

THE AROMA OF PROGRESS

Eventually, if you stay with it, you'll notice something shift. The aroma begins to waft through your life. Progress becomes visible. What felt like invisible simmering starts to reveal itself as transformation.

You may not see it day to day. But one day you'll look back and realize: the waiting wasn't wasted. Every day you showed up, every doubt you worked through, every moment you chose to continue—it was all building toward this.

Take a deep breath. Get started. And when the middle feels endless, remember: the simmering is where the flavor develops. Stay with the pot.

Intention of the Day

I will commit fully to the process of what matters to me, trusting it is worth it.

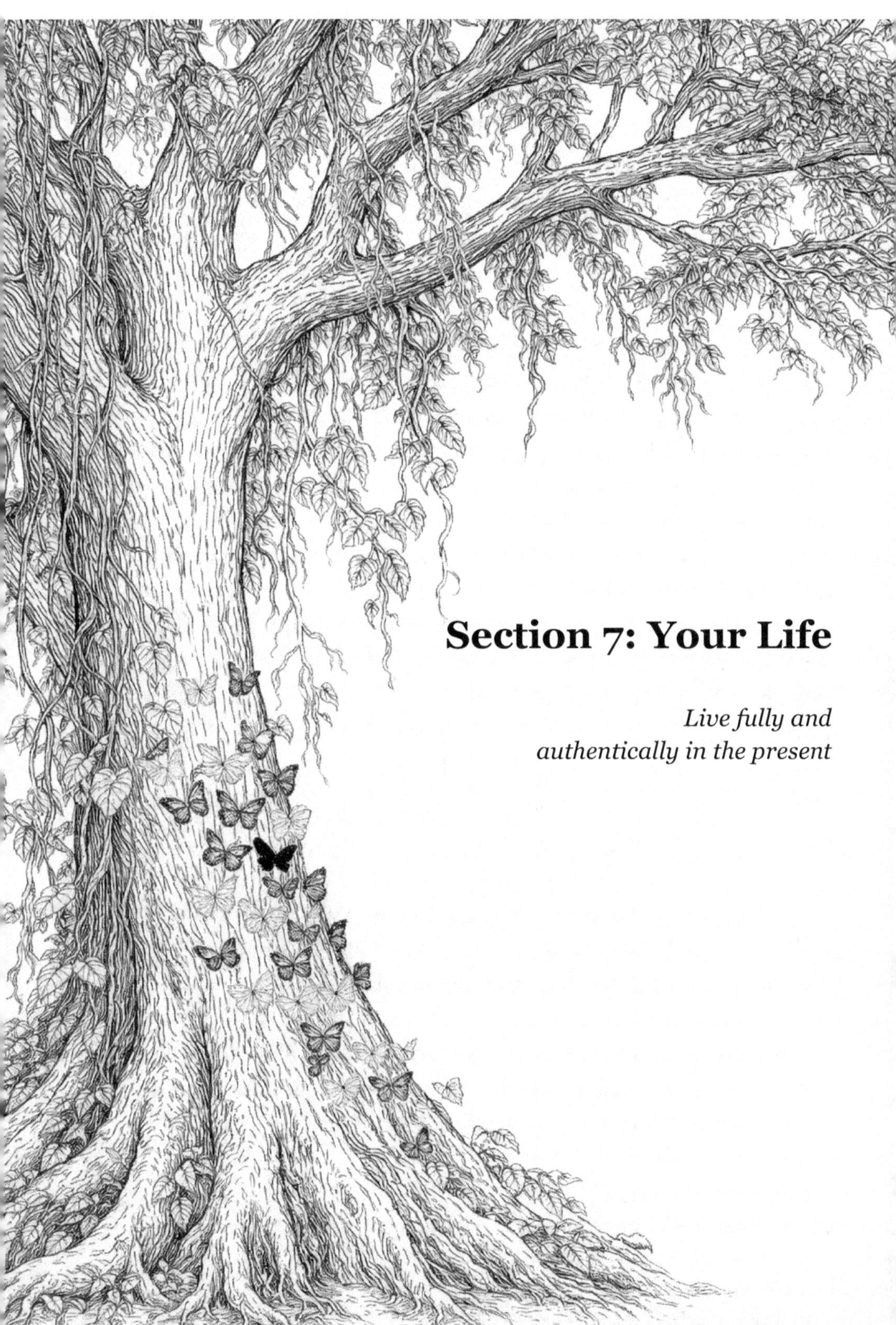

Section 7: Your Life

*Live fully and
authentically in the present*

Take Your Time

You've learned to recognize your Authentic Self, distinguish it from your Created Self, and identify your purpose. You've gathered tools for caring for your body, examining your beliefs, processing trauma, and building your tribe. Now comes the practice of bringing all of this into your daily life—not just in purpose-work, but in every moment. That practice begins with the hardest thing for most of us: slowing down enough to notice what matters.

When going through life at light speed, there's a lot that can pass you by. Not just opportunities for seeing the sights. It's much more than that.

Moving too fast, you might miss subtle physical cues that your body is not feeling well. You might overlook your loved one's demeanor that suggests they are sad and need comfort. You could skim past a notice in the corner of your cable bill warning that monthly charges are about to increase. You might rush through a chai latte without noticing how much tastier it is when you're not gulping it down.

And you might miss moments that connect you to who you are.

Whenever I visited my grandfather as a child, he always gave me a Werther's Original hard candy. It was a small ritual, but it meant the world to me. Now, whenever I see the Werther's commercial showing an elderly man giving a hard candy to his grandchild, I think of him. That moment of recognition—that brief pause where past and present meet— only happens when I'm moving slowly enough to notice.

Your Created Self thrives on speed and productivity. It measures worth by how much you accomplish. But your Authentic Self needs stillness to be heard. It speaks in quiet moments, in sensory details, in memories triggered by unexpected connections. When you rush through life, you miss its voice.

Modern society is fast-paced. Still, find time to slow down so that you can see, hear, feel, taste, smell, and remember the full richness of life. These moments remind you why it's worth living.

Intention of the Day
I will slow down today so I can notice what I would otherwise miss.

Anchors to the Present

Living the adult life is truly a test. Your energy and attention are constantly pulled toward the past—its comforts and regrets—and toward the future—its worries and hopes. Meanwhile, the present moment feels overwhelming with responsibilities, relationships, and the demands of daily life.

Your mind does what minds do when overwhelmed—it tries to escape. It runs to the past, clinging to memories or replaying old wounds. When that becomes painful, it runs to the future, worrying about what might happen. Back and forth, trying to avoid the unbearable present.

Your Authentic Self lives in the present moment. It doesn't dwell in yesterday's mistakes or tomorrow's anxieties. Your Created Self, on the other hand, tends to pull you backward and forward—replaying old wounds, rehearsing future conversations, worrying about things that haven't happened yet. This mental time travel drains you without accomplishing anything.

The good news? You don't have to force your way back to presence through sheer willpower. Nature and simple physical anchors can bring you home.

NATURE'S GIFT OF PRESENCE

Endless brain chatter. The monkey mind racing a mile a minute. Our minds are constantly planning, problem-solving, and worrying. What needs to be done, when it must be done, who we need to talk to about it. The mental noise can feel overwhelming.

Then something shifts. Nature interrupts.

You see a big, beautiful monarch butterfly pass by your window. For that moment, your mind goes completely quiet. Nothing else exists except that butterfly.

Or maybe it's the soothing sound of light rain dancing on your rooftop. The gentle cool breeze brushing across your skin on a warm, sunny day. The gloriously bright full moon lighting the clouds and treetops at night. Whatever the moment, your mind stops chattering. You become fully present.

And what is your mind doing during those moments? Absolutely nothing.

This is nature's gift—moments of complete presence when your Authentic Self can simply be. No planning, no worry, no mental noise. Just existence. Whether it's for five seconds or fifty minutes, nature blesses us with these pauses to help us find calm, beauty, and peace in the midst of our madness.

The remarkable thing is that these moments are free and always available. You don't need a beach vacation or a mountain retreat. Nature's gifts show up in everyday life if you pay attention.

LIVING BEINGS AS ANCHORS

I experience presence most fully when I'm with animals. Whether I'm brushing a cat, hand-feeding a guinea pig, or playing keep-away with a dog who has a ball in their mouth, I am completely in the moment. There's no room for worry about the past or future when a playful dog is daring me to catch them. Animals live entirely in the present, and spending time with them invites me to do the same.

This isn't just about pets. Watching children play, observing birds at a feeder, even noticing an ant carrying a crumb—any living being fully engaged in their moment can call you into yours.

PHYSICAL ANCHORS WHEN NATURE ISN'T AVAILABLE

When nature isn't immediately available and you need to return to presence, your body offers reliable anchors. Try this: place one hand on your chest and take three slow breaths, noticing the rise and fall beneath your palm. Feel your feet on the floor. Notice one thing you can see right now, one sound you can hear, one sensation you can feel. These simple acts anchor you here.

Your breath is always with you. Three conscious breaths—inhaling slowly, exhaling fully—can interrupt the spiral and bring you back. Your body in space is always with you. Feeling your feet on the ground, your sit bones on the chair, your hands resting in your lap—these sensations exist only in the present moment.

Finding Your Anchors

Different anchors work for different people and different moments. Some days, stepping outside and noticing the temperature on your skin brings you back. Other days, petting your cat or watching clouds shift across the sky. Still others, the simple act of drinking water slowly and noticing the sensation.

Find what brings you into the present. When you notice your mind wandering into past or future, gently bring your attention back using whatever anchor feels available. This isn't about perfection—your mind will wander thousands of times. What matters is the practice of returning, again and again, to where you actually are.

Protect your energy by staying present as often as you can. Your peace, happiness, and clarity depend on it. So when you feel lost, alone, or overwhelmed, seek out nature intentionally. Watch the clouds from your window. Admire a flower on your desk. Play with your pet. Even watching videos of puppies and kittens counts—nature takes many forms. The key is giving yourself permission to pause and let the present moment quiet your mind.

Your Authentic Self knows this kind of rest is essential. Let nature and simple presence be your wise and loving companion through life.

Intention of the Day
I will use one anchor today to bring myself back to the present moment.

Live with Gratitude

Gratitude shifts your focus from what's missing to what's present. It doesn't deny difficulties—it acknowledges what sustains you through them.

Your Created Self was trained to scan for problems, inadequacies, and threats. That's how it keeps you "safe"—by staying vigilant about what could go wrong or what you lack. This constant scanning creates a mental habit of noticing what's missing, what's broken, what needs fixing.

Your Authentic Self knows a different truth: you can acknowledge difficulty and simultaneously recognize what's working, what's nourishing you, what's already good. This isn't toxic positivity—it's seeing the whole picture instead of only the problems.

HOW GRATITUDE REWIRES YOUR ATTENTION

Your brain has a negativity bias—it's wired to notice and remember threats more than comforts. This kept our ancestors alive when danger lurked around every corner. But in modern life, this bias means you can experience ninety-nine good moments and one bad one, and your mind fixates on the bad.

Gratitude practice doesn't erase the bad moment. It trains your attention to also notice the ninety-nine good ones. Over time, this rewiring changes your baseline experience of life. You still see problems clearly—you just stop seeing only problems.

GRATITUDE AS SELF-CARE

When you practice gratitude, you're not performing positivity for others. You're caring for your own nervous system. Noticing what's working calms the part of your brain that's constantly scanning for danger. It tells your body: in this moment, you're okay. This small shift—from scanning for threats to noticing support—is foundational self-care.

This matters especially during hard times. When life feels overwhelming, gratitude doesn't minimize your struggle. It reminds you that you're not only struggling—you're also breathing, you have shelter, you experienced one kind word today. These aren't small things. They're the foundation you're standing on while you face what's hard.

WHAT GRATITUDE LOOKS LIKE

Gratitude doesn't require grand gestures or perfect circumstances. It lives in small, specific moments:

- I am grateful for the hot cup of tea that starts my day on a warm note.

- I am grateful for family and friends with whom I share love, support, memories, and courage.
- I am grateful for my clothes that are clean, comfortable, and protect my body.
- I am grateful for the food that nourishes my body and fuels my day.
- I am grateful for working from home with the forty-minute commute time gifted back to me each morning and afternoon.
- I am grateful for employment that supports my survival and livelihood.
- I am grateful for birds singing, because it soothes my soul.
- I am grateful for my collection of crystals, because they reflect the beauty of nature.
- I am grateful for dogs and cats, because they give instant presence and unconditional love.
- I am grateful for meditation for helping me ground and center at the beginning and end of each day.
- I am grateful for my bed that provides comfort, support, security, and care while I rest and restore.

Notice how specific these are. "I'm grateful for my job" becomes "I'm grateful for working from home with forty minutes gifted back each day." The specificity matters—it anchors gratitude in real, lived experience rather than abstract obligation.

Building the Practice

You don't need to feel grateful to practice gratitude. Start where you are. Notice one thing today—just one. Tomorrow, notice another. The practice isn't about forcing positive feelings. It's about paying attention to what's already present.

Some people keep gratitude journals. Some say three things aloud each morning. Some pause before meals to acknowledge what made the food possible. Some text a friend one thing they appreciated about their day. The method doesn't matter. What matters is consistency—returning again and again to the practice of noticing what's good alongside what's hard.

What are you grateful for today? Start small. Notice one thing. Let that be enough.

Intention of the Day
I will practice gratitude today so that I remember what's already good in my life.

Laugh

When was the last time you truly laughed? Not a polite chuckle, but a bust-a-gut, crying, barely-able-to-stand kind of laugh. The kind where your face contorts, your throat constricts, and your abdominal muscles squeeze the air out of you. That sounds almost painful—so why do we enjoy it so much?

Because of the release.

Laughter purges negative and unwanted emotions from your body. Those muscles gripping you are squeezing out irritability, sorrow, worry, and anger. As they release, they make room for joy, excitement, love, and bliss to enter. That final breath of relief at the end—ahhh—is your body resetting itself.

This isn't just a feeling. Research shows that laughter triggers the release of endorphins—your body's natural painkillers and mood elevators. It reduces stress hormones, improves circulation, and even boosts immune function. When you laugh deeply, your nervous system shifts from stress to rest. Your body literally heals itself through joy.

I experienced this when Hurricane Melissa was heading toward Jamaica in October 2025—the strongest recorded hurricane in Atlantic history. As people prepared for the storm, I felt heavy with worry and despair for my country, my people, and especially my family. Then, while scrolling through Instagram, I saw a video of a man lying on top of his roof in Jamaica. He was caressing the roof gently. He said he was spending some quality time with it before Melissa took it away.

I burst out laughing. The comments made it even better—one person told him to write his name on the roof so somebody could bring it back to him.

That video embodied a truth Jamaicans have always known: tek bad tings mek joke—take the bad things and make jokes from them. This isn't denial or avoidance. It's a survival skill passed down through generations. When life hands you a Category 5 hurricane, sometimes the healthiest response is dark humor and community laughter.

This cultural wisdom recognizes something profound: you can acknowledge the seriousness of a situation and still find room for lightness. The man on the roof wasn't pretending the hurricane wasn't coming. He was choosing how to spend the hours before it arrived—connected to his community through shared laughter rather than isolated in fear.

Your Created Self might insist that laughing when things are serious is inappropriate or irresponsible. It learned that serious situations demand serious faces. But your Authentic Self knows better. Laughter doesn't minimize your problems—it gives you strength to face them. It reminds you that even in darkness, light can break through.

In that moment watching the video, I remembered that in times of adversity, a little comedy helps you get through. The worry didn't disappear, but the laughter made room for hope alongside it.

Find a way to laugh today. Share a joke with someone you love. Watch a comedy. Reminisce about something funny that happened to you. Scroll through videos that make you smile. It doesn't matter how big or small the laugh is. It will make room for some good energy in your soul.

And when life gets difficult—because it will—remember: tek bad tings mek joke. You're not being callous. You're being resilient.

Intention of the Day
I will find a reason to laugh today so I can make room for joy.

Fond Memories

Yesterday was a day. A day of being dismissed, misunderstood, disappointed, angry, and irritated. Then, while meditating that evening, a memory surfaced that shifted everything.

I was pet sitting for a friend. His older dog, Kenya, wasn't in the kitchen with the younger two when I arrived. I called out, asking where their brother was. Suddenly I heard him running—fast—down the stairs. My heart raced. I thought he'd mistaken me for an intruder. But the moment Kenya saw me, his ears dropped, his tail wagged, and he trotted over happily. I laughed out loud at how frightened I'd been over nothing.

That one memory turned my whole day around.

WHY MEMORIES MATTER FOR YOUR AUTHENTIC SELF

Good memories, no matter how few, play a big role in keeping us on the right track. They remind us of what is possible in the world. They show us how good life can be and inspire us to work toward that feeling again. Good memories nourish the good that lives in each of us, especially when we doubt that any good remains.

But there's something deeper happening when you recall a fond memory. Those moments aren't just pleasant nostalgia—they're proof of who you really are.

Your Created Self is shaped by criticism, fear, and adaptation to others' expectations. It carries the voice that says you're not enough, that you always mess up, that you should be ashamed. When life is hard, your Created Self gets louder, drowning out everything else.

Your Authentic Self is revealed in your fond memories. The person who laughed with genuine delight at a misunderstanding with a dog. The person who felt loved receiving a piece of candy from their grandfather. The person who helped a stranger and felt their heart open. These memories aren't accidents—they're glimpses of who you actually are beneath all the conditioning.

When you're struggling, fond memories become evidence that contradicts what your Created Self is telling you. You're not fundamentally broken. You're not incapable of joy. You're not unworthy of love. The proof lives in your memories of moments when you were whole, happy, and exactly yourself.

THE PRACTICE: KEEP PROOF OF GOOD

Start collecting evidence of your Authentic Self. This doesn't mean pretending hard things didn't happen or that pain doesn't exist. It means balancing the record.

Your Created Self keeps meticulous records of every failure, every rejection, every time you fell short. It replays these on loop, building a case that you should stay small, stay safe, stay afraid.

Your Authentic Self needs its own file—moments that prove who you really are:

- Times you showed up for someone even when it was hard
- Moments of unexpected joy or laughter
- Instances when you chose kindness over judgment
- Days when you tried something new despite fear
- Memories of connection, play, delight, courage, love

Start collecting evidence of your Authentic Self. Write down fond memories. Keep a note on your phone of moments when you felt truly yourself. When your Created Self starts its chorus of criticism, pull out your evidence. That version of you in the good memory? That's the real you. The rest is just weather passing through.

WHEN SOMEONE MAKES YOU FEEL SMALL

When someone makes you feel less than whole, remember the person who made you feel like a gift. When something goes wrong, remember a day when everything went right. When your heart feels heavy, remember what makes it sing.

Those fond memories are telling you something important: you were, are, and will always be a life worth living. The hard days are real. So are the good moments. Both are true. Your Authentic Self knows how to hold both at once.

Intention of the Day
I will recall a fond memory today so that I remember who I truly am.

Seasonal Self-Care

Your self-care needs are not static. They shift with the seasons—and fighting that rhythm drains energy better spent adapting.

In winter, daylight shrinks and temperatures drop. Your body naturally craves more rest, warming foods, and indoor comfort. In summer, longer days invite movement, lighter meals, and time outside. Spring and fall are transitions—your needs may fluctuate as your body adjusts to changing light and temperature. These shifts aren't weakness or inconsistency. They're your Authentic Self responding to the world around you.

I experience this tension every year. I have severe seasonal allergies, particularly in spring. I can't walk outside when pollen counts spike. I also avoid outdoor walks in winter because of the cold. Finding cardio that doesn't require commuting somewhere—or walking in place at home, which I have no interest in—becomes frustrating. I volunteer walking dogs at the shelter, but I skip spring due to allergies and summer due to mosquitoes. Six months pass without volunteering, and I have to re-register every year. The disruption to routines I love used to frustrate me deeply.

What helped was reframing seasons as invitations rather than obstacles. Spring and summer aren't failing me by triggering allergies. Winter isn't punishing me with cold. Each season simply asks for a different version of self-care. When I stopped expecting my routines to stay constant year-round, the frustration softened.

HONORING SEASONAL SHIFTS

Here's how your self-care might adapt across seasons:

Energy and rest. Winter's shorter days naturally signal more rest. Rather than forcing summer-level productivity, honor your body's need to slow down. In summer, longer light supports more activity—take advantage of that energy while it's available.

Light exposure. In darker months, prioritize morning light to regulate your internal clock. Open blinds immediately upon waking. Consider a light therapy lamp if winter affects your mood. In summer, balance light exposure with protecting your sleep—dim screens and lights as evening approaches.

Sleep patterns. Your sleep needs may increase in winter and decrease in summer. Rather than rigidly maintaining the same schedule year-round, notice what your body actually asks for. As you learned in "Self-Care Tip: Sleep Hygiene," consistency matters—but consistency can flex with the seasons.

Movement. Outdoor movement isn't always possible. In challenging seasons, explore indoor alternatives that genuinely appeal to you—dancing in your living room, online yoga classes, or strength training at home. The goal isn't maintaining identical routines but staying active in ways that fit current conditions.

Nutrition. Your body often craves warming, grounding foods in winter—soups, stews, root vegetables—and lighter, cooling foods in summer—salads, fresh fruits, smoothies. Trust these cravings as wisdom rather than fighting them with rigid meal plans that ignore the season.

Beyond Weather: Life's Cyclical Rhythms

The principle of seasonal self-care extends beyond calendar seasons. If you work in education, your energy demands shift dramatically between semesters and breaks. If you work retail or delivery, holiday seasons require different self-care than slower months. If you travel predictably for work or family, those rhythms deserve their own adaptations.

Whatever cycles shape your life—weather, work, school, caregiving—your Authentic Self knows that needs shift. Honoring those shifts isn't inconsistency. It's wisdom.

For Readers in Different Climates

If you live in a tropical climate without dramatic seasonal changes, your rhythms may follow rainy and dry seasons, hurricane seasons, or cultural calendars rather than temperature shifts. The principle remains: notice when your environment changes and adapt your self-care accordingly. Your Authentic Self responds to the world around you, wherever you are.

Seasons aren't obstacles to your self-care routine. They're invitations to practice flexibility, presence, and trust in your body's wisdom. What worked last month may not work this month—and that's not failure. That's living in rhythm with life itself.

Intention of the Day
I will notice what this season asks of me so that my self-care honors where I am right now.

Self-Care During Major Life Transitions

Life transitions—job changes, moves, relationship shifts, new parenthood, loss—disrupt everything. Your routines fall apart. Your energy scatters. The self-care practices that once grounded you may suddenly feel impossible or irrelevant. This is normal. And being gentle with yourself during upheaval is essential.

Your Created Self may insist you should handle transitions smoothly. It compares you to others who seem to navigate change effortlessly. It pushes you to maintain your usual productivity, routines, and composure—even when everything around you is shifting. But your Authentic Self knows the truth: transitions require different care than stable seasons. Forcing normalcy during upheaval only adds exhaustion to an already demanding time.

THE BASICS MATTER MOST

When life is in flux, return to fundamentals. Sleep, hydration, and nourishment become your anchors. You may not have energy for your full self-care routine—and that's okay. Protecting the basics keeps you functioning while everything else settles.

As you learned in "Know Your Limits Before You Cross Them," understanding your capacity helps you set realistic expectations. During transitions, your capacity is reduced. Adjust accordingly. What you could handle last month may be too much right now.

JOB TRANSITIONS

Changing jobs is harder than it looks. Leaving a position well means offloading responsibilities, tying up loose ends, and preserving your reputation in the industry. Starting a new role means orientation, paperwork, tax forms, benefits enrollment, and meeting everyone you'll work with. Both ends of the transition demand significant energy.

I learned this the hard way. Whenever I didn't take time off between ending one job and starting another, I arrived at the new position already exhausted. Now I try to take at least three days between jobs—ideally a week. I frame that time as celebration for finishing the old chapter and rest in preparation for the new one. I also use it to acclimate to routine changes, like waking an hour earlier or shifting my bedtime. That buffer transforms the transition from depleting to sustainable.

If taking time off isn't financially possible, be especially protective of evenings and weekends during the overlap. Treat rest as non-negotiable rather than optional.

RELOCATING

Moving disrupts nearly every dimension of your health at once. Your environment changes completely. Your routines dissolve. Your social connections may be left behind. Even positive relocations—moving for a dream job, a better climate, or to be closer to family—carry grief for what you're leaving.

During a move, give yourself permission for things to be chaotic. Boxes may sit unpacked for weeks. You may eat takeout more than usual. Your exercise routine may disappear temporarily. This isn't failure—it's triage. Focus on creating one small anchor in your new space as quickly as possible: a corner that feels like yours, a morning ritual you can maintain, a walking route you'll learn. These small consistencies help your nervous system settle while everything else remains in flux.

Rebuilding your tribe takes time. You won't replace years of friendship in the first month. Be patient with the loneliness that often accompanies relocation and intentional about seeking connection—even small interactions with neighbors, coworkers, or local shopkeepers help you feel less untethered.

OTHER TRANSITIONS

Whatever transition you're facing—new parenthood, divorce, caring for aging parents, a health diagnosis, retirement, or loss—the principles remain the same. Protect the basics. Lower your expectations temporarily. Recognize that your routines may need to be rebuilt rather than maintained. Lean on your tribe, as you explored in "Your Tribe Is Self-Care." And as you learned in "Be Realistic," set goals that honor your current reality rather than your ideal circumstances.

If a transition triggers something deeper—persistent hopelessness, inability to function, or thoughts of self-harm—please turn to "Self-Care Tip: When to Seek Professional Help." Some transitions require professional support, and recognizing that is wisdom, not weakness.

YOUR AUTHENTIC SELF REMAINS

Transitions can make you feel like you've lost yourself. Your routines are gone. Your environment may be unfamiliar. Your energy is depleted. But your Authentic Self is still there—beneath the chaos, beneath the exhaustion, waiting for things to settle enough to be heard again.

Give yourself grace. Transitions end. Routines rebuild. You will find your footing. Until then, care for yourself with the same compassion you'd offer a dear friend navigating upheaval.

Intention of the Day
I will be gentle with myself today so that I have grace for whatever transition I'm navigating.

Finding Meaning in Every Moment

In "Lessons in the Negative," you explored how major adversity—career crises, business struggles, life upheavals—can clarify your purpose. This article is about something smaller but equally important: finding meaning and unexpected beauty in the ordinary moments of daily life.

When small things don't go according to plan—a delayed train, a rainy day that cancels your picnic, a long line at the grocery store—it's easy to get caught up in frustration. Your Created Self immediately labels these moments as "bad" and spirals into irritation about lost time or ruined plans. But what if these ordinary inconveniences held something valuable?

THE CHALLENGE OF AUTOMATIC INTERPRETATION

Your neighbor's dog barks early every morning, waking you before your alarm. Your Created Self labels this as an annoyance, another thing wrong with your day before it's even begun.

Your Authentic Self can pause and ask: What's actually happening here? The dog is simply being a dog. And you're awake—with unexpected quiet time before the rush begins. What might you do with these extra minutes that you wouldn't otherwise have?

It's perfectly fine to feel annoyed by inconveniences. Living mindfully is knowing how to eventually find value in moments your Created Self wants to dismiss.

FINDING BEAUTY IN THE ORDINARY

Seeing lots of trash in a pond creates disappointment about pollution and harm to the environment. But pause longer. Notice how the light catches the water's surface anyway. Watch the dragonfly hovering above it, unbothered. See the turtle sunning itself on a log despite everything. Beauty and brokenness coexist. Your Created Self sees only the trash. Your Authentic Self can hold both truths at once—acknowledging what's wrong while still noticing what's beautiful.

A rainstorm ruins your outdoor plans. But have you stood at the window and really watched rain? The way it moves in sheets, the sound it makes on different surfaces, the green it brings out in the leaves? Your

Created Self sees a cancelled afternoon. Your Authentic Self might discover unexpected stillness.

FINDING VALUE IN WAITING

Do you remember waiting for something and finding that the anticipation made the arrival sweeter?

Consider how technology has changed our relationship with waiting. Years ago, connecting to the internet required patience. You would hear the sounds of the connection being made, wait through each step, and feel a small surge of satisfaction when it finally worked. Today, everything is instantaneous. We've gained speed, but we've lost something too—those built-in pauses that gave our minds a chance to breathe and our hearts a moment to anticipate.

In Jamaica, movie theaters still have intermission. The film pauses halfway through, and the lights come up. At first, this might seem like an inconvenience. But I've come to appreciate what it offers. Intermission gives me a chance to visit the restroom and grab snacks without missing anything. More importantly, it provides an opportunity to talk with my friends or family about what we've seen so far and to build anticipation for what's to come. By the time the lights dim again, we're more engaged than we would have been without the pause.

Your Created Self craves instant results. It wants to skip ahead to the destination without experiencing the journey. But your Authentic Self understands that pauses and waiting have value. They create space for reflection, anticipation, and appreciation. They allow you to savor what's coming instead of rushing past it.

THE PRACTICE: PAUSE, OBSERVE, ASK

Whether it's finding a lesson in frustration or beauty in something broken, holding space between stimulus and reaction makes the difference between having a bad moment and having a meaningful one— between rushing through life and savoring it.

When something small doesn't go as planned, try this:

Pause: Take one breath before reacting.

Observe: Notice what actually happened, separate from your interpretation of what it means.

Ask: What might this teach me? What beauty or value exists here that I'm missing because I'm focused only on the problem?

Not every delay is frustrating. Some are invitations to be present. Not every inconvenience is an obstacle. Some are doorways to noticing what you'd otherwise miss. Not every imperfect moment is ruined. Some hold unexpected gifts.

Take advantage of the pauses and anticipation along your journey. Notice what lessons live in small frustrations. Find what beauty exists in ordinary moments. They make room for more satisfaction, wisdom, and joy—not just when you finally arrive, but right now.

Intention of the Day
I will pause before reacting today so that I can find the meaning in what happened.

Make Room for Happiness

Think of a puppy learning to walk down a flight of stairs. At first, the puppy is fearful, whimpering at the top while you stand at the bottom encouraging them. They observe you descend safely a few times. They want desperately to reach you. Finally, they brave those stairs—slowly, clumsily, even tumbling down the last few steps. But they make it to the bottom and run happily into your loving hands.

The puppy didn't wait until the fear disappeared. The puppy moved through the fear because something better was waiting on the other side.

THE ADULT VERSION OF THE STAIRS

When we face the barriers of adult life—difficult relationships, unexpected losses, health struggles, financial uncertainty—it's tempting to remain frozen at the top of the stairs. Grief, confusion, helplessness, and anger can feel safer than the work required to move through them. The descent appears steep. The steps feel uncertain. Part of you would rather remain where you are than risk stumbling.

This is your Created Self attempting to protect you. It prefers the familiar discomfort of staying stuck over the unfamiliar territory of healing. It knows the pain you're in, and that feels safer than the unknown of what comes after. The Created Self whispers: What if you do all this work and it doesn't get better? What if you risk vulnerability and get hurt again? What if you let go of this pain and there's nothing on the other side?

But your Authentic Self recognizes something important: you cannot reach peace by avoiding pain. You have to move through it.

WHAT THE STAIRS ACTUALLY ARE

For adult readers, the "stairs" aren't literal. They're the emotional and psychological work you've been learning throughout this book:

- The grief you explored in Section 4 that still needs feeling
- The anger you've been holding that needs release
- The fear that keeps you playing small
- The past wounds that convinced you staying stuck is safer than healing
- The boundaries you need to set but keep avoiding
- The forgiveness work you know would free you but feels impossible

Each step down requires using tools you've learned: grounding when panic rises, breathing when your body tenses, reaching for your tribe when loneliness tempts you to quit, trusting your Authentic Self when your Created Self screams to go back up.

PRACTICAL STEPS FOR DESCENDING

You don't have to do this perfectly. The puppy tumbled down the last few steps and still made it. Here's how to start:

- **Name what you're at the top of.** What specific pain or pattern are you trying to move through? Grief over a loss? Fear of being alone? Shame about a past mistake? Clarity helps.

- **Identify your first step.** Not the whole staircase—just the first step. Maybe it's: "I will journal about this for ten minutes." Or "I will tell one person how I actually feel." Or "I will sit with this emotion for five minutes without distracting myself."

- **Use your tools.** You've learned grounding techniques, breathing practices, and ways to process difficult emotions. Pick one tool and use it as you take that first step. The Mind-Body Connection scan. The 3-Step Reality Check for questioning beliefs. The Delay-Distract-Decide technique for impulse control. Your self-care toolkit is full—use it.

- **Let your tribe spot you.** The puppy wouldn't have descended if no one was waiting at the bottom. Your tribe is there. Tell someone you're working through something hard. You don't have to do this alone.

- **Expect stumbling.** You will not descend gracefully. Some days you'll take three steps down and slide back two. That's not failure—that's the process. The puppy tumbled. You will too. What matters is continuing downward.

- **Remember what's waiting.** At the bottom of these stairs: hope, joy, connection, freedom. The version of you who isn't controlled by this pain. The life where this wound doesn't run the show. Keep that image clear. It's what pulls you forward when fear tries to push you back.

YOU'VE DONE THIS BEFORE

You have already survived difficult descents before - even if you don't fully recognize them yet. Think about your own life. Maybe you left a relationship or job that was draining you. Maybe you set a boundary when it felt impossible. Maybe you've worked through grief, let go of anger, or stopped believing something that was holding you back. Maybe you're facing that challenge right now. Whatever your stairs look like, you have evidence in your own life that difficult things can be survived.

Trust that evidence. Trust your Authentic Self to guide you down these stairs, however long it takes. You may move slowly. You may stumble. But each step forward creates space for happiness to enter.

The beauty waiting at the bottom—peace, joy, connection, freedom—doesn't appear until you take the first step. And then the next.

Peace is waiting. Start moving toward it.

Intention of the Day
I will move through difficult emotions so I create space for happiness to enter.

You Are Never Alone

Sometimes life gets so busy that you forget you're part of something larger. Stress piles up. Days pass without meaningful connection to others. You might go weeks without truly engaging with your tribe. And slowly, without realizing it, you start to feel like you're the only one carrying whatever burden weighs on you.

That loneliness can convince you that no one else understands what you're going through. The uncomfortable thoughts, feelings, and emotions you're experiencing start to feel uniquely yours—as if you're alone in the struggle.

You're not.

Remember the energy body you learned about earlier? That system of pure energy connects you not just to your own well-being but to every living thing around you. All life shares this energy. The trees outside your window, the birds in the sky, the people across the world experiencing their own challenges right now—you are part of a collective that has always included you, even when you've forgotten.

When stress or time alone blocks your awareness of this connection, you can clear the way back to it. Try this: close your eyes and take a few slow, deep breaths at your own pace. With each inhale, imagine drawing in calm, bright energy from the world around you. With each exhale, release whatever heaviness you've been carrying. Let it go, trusting that it will be cleansed and transformed. After a few breaths, take a moment to feel gratitude for the energy you just received and for the reminder that you belong to something vast and loving.

This practice doesn't change your circumstances. But it can shift how alone you feel within them. You are always connected to the collective—even when life makes you forget.

Intention of the Day
I will pause to feel my connection to all life so I remember I belong.

Self-Care Tip: Connect with your Ancestors

Whether you were close to them or never met them, whether they passed long ago or are still living, your ancestors got you here. Whether they set great examples or were deeply flawed, they offered life lessons and provided stories for future generations. Connecting with them is a form of self-care that grounds you in something larger than yourself.

When I look at my family, I see where different parts of me come from. My paternal great-grandfather, my maternal grandparents, and my father were all business owners. I get my business sense from them. My mother and paternal grandmother were nurses, and my maternal grandmother was a nurses' aide. I get my care for others from them. My maternal grandmother was "of the earth," picking and roasting her own coffee beans to make her coffee. I get my love of the land from her. My mother has a beautiful garden at home with bougainvillea, snake plants, bird of paradise, red ixora, orchids, and anthurium. I get my green thumb from her.

Seeing these links helps me understand myself. The traits I carry aren't random. They're gifts passed down through generations, shaped by people who faced their own challenges and found their own ways to thrive.

There are many ways to connect with your ancestors. Ask living relatives to share stories about family members who came before. Look through old photos and notice faces or expressions you recognize. Research where your family came from. Cook recipes that have been passed down. Visit places where your ancestors lived or worked. Or simply pause to feel gratitude for all that you are because of them.

Your ancestors shaped who you are. Honoring them honors yourself.

Self-Care Tip: Use Your Hands

Your hands are remarkable tools. They allow you to create physical versions of your thoughts, ideas, and emotions. They help you survive daily life, but they also give you room to express yourself, create beauty, and have fun.

Using your hands for creative or tactile work offers benefits beyond the finished product. It reduces stress by focusing your mind on a single task. It brings you into the present moment, quieting the mental chatter that pulls you into past or future. It provides a sense of accomplishment when you complete something tangible. And it connects you to your Authentic Self by allowing you to express who you are through what you make.

I discovered this through knitting. As I shared earlier in "Worry Reveals Opportunity," what began as a practical solution to cold Connecticut winters became a 25-year practice. But knitting gave me more than warm clothes—it became a form of meditation and self-expression. The repetitive motion calms my mind. The finished hats, scarves, and sweaters remind me of what I'm capable of creating. And every gift I knit for someone carries a piece of my care and attention.

Think about how much time your hands spend typing and tapping on devices. Consider giving them something different to do today. Make pottery or bake bread. Knit or crochet a gift for someone you love. Paint, sculpt, or try woodworking. Arrange flowers or repot a plant. Give your partner a five-minute back rub.

It doesn't matter what you choose. What matters is that you're using your hands to express your creativity, your feelings, and your Authentic Self. The simple act of making something with your hands can restore a sense of connection to yourself that screens often take away.

Brighten Someone's Day

Small acts of kindness carry more weight than you might realize. A single moment of care can shift someone's entire day—and that shift ripples outward. The person you helped treats the next person a little better. That person does the same. What started as one small gesture becomes a wave of good moving through the world.

You already have what it takes to start that wave.

Think about the tools that have helped you on your journey. Maybe meditation quieted your mind when nothing else could. Maybe journaling helped you process emotions you didn't know how to name. Maybe a breathing exercise brought you back to calm during a hard moment. These aren't just tools for you—they're gifts you can share.

When someone tells you they're struggling to let go of anger or hurt, you don't have to have all the answers. But you can share what worked for you. "Have you tried journaling about it?" or "There's a breathing exercise that helped me—want me to show you?" This isn't about obligation. Your Created Self might read "brighten someone's day" as another task on an endless list of what you should do for others. That's not what this is. When you've filled your own cup—when you've practiced authentic self-care and connected with your Authentic Self—kindness flows naturally outward. It's not effort. It's overflow.

Beyond sharing tools, consider the small gestures that require almost no effort but mean so much. Send an unexpected text to check in on a friend. Not because they asked, but because you thought of them. That one message might arrive at exactly the moment they needed to feel less alone.

Your Authentic Self knows that brightening someone else's day also brightens your own. Giving and receiving aren't separate—they're part of the same flow. When you help others heal, you reinforce your own healing. When you offer kindness, you remind yourself that kindness exists.

Go brighten someone's day today. You might just brighten your own.

Intention of the Day
I will share something helpful with someone today so that kindness ripples outward.

Oneness through Love

L ove isn't just about romance, family, and friends. You might reserve the word "love" for your closest relationships—partners, children, parents, best friends. But love is much bigger than that. Love is recognizing another person as a soul living the human experience, just like you. It's seeing the cashier, the bus driver, and the stranger on the street as beings with their own fears, hopes, and struggles. When you understand this, something shifts. You realize you're connected to everyone.

Your Created Self and Separation

Your Created Self was built on separation. It learned to categorize people: safe or dangerous, valuable or worthless, like me or not like me. This categorizing served a purpose—it helped you navigate a complex social world and identify your tribe. But it also created walls. It made you believe that some people matter more than others. That some deserve compassion while others don't. That love must be earned, deserved, or restricted to the worthy.

Your Authentic Self knows differently. It recognizes that every soul has equal value—not because of what they achieve, what they look like, or how they treat you, but simply because they exist. This isn't naive. You can recognize someone's inherent worth while also setting boundaries against their harmful behavior. Love doesn't mean tolerating harm. It means seeing the humanity in everyone, including those who've lost sight of their own.

What Expanded Love Looks Like

This expanded love shows up in simple ways. It's showing goodwill toward people you'll never see again. It's noticing how your energy affects someone's comfort or mood. It's pausing to consider how your actions might impact others, both now and later. It's trying to understand someone's perspective even when you disagree. It's accepting differences you don't fully understand and choosing respect anyway.

Above all, this love remembers that no one is of greater or lesser value than another. Not the CEO, not the janitor. Not your neighbor, not the person across the world. Every soul has equal worth. When you hold this truth, judgment softens. Compassion grows. The barriers between "us" and "them" begin to dissolve.

Living From This Understanding

You practice this love when you make eye contact with the checkout clerk and actually see them. When you let someone merge in traffic without resentment. When you hold the door for the person behind you. When you offer directions to someone who's lost. When you choose patience with the customer service representative who's just doing their job.

These aren't grand gestures. They're small recognitions that the person in front of you is human—tired, trying, worthy of basic kindness. When you approach interactions this way, you're not performing goodness for others to witness. You're living from your Authentic Self, which already knows: we're all connected. We're all struggling. We're all doing our best with what we have.

The Practice

Start small. Today, practice this expanded love with one person outside your inner circle. The person who delivers your mail. The stranger you pass on your walk. The barista making your coffee. See them as fully human—someone with a history, with worries, with people who love them, with dreams they're working toward or have given up on.

You don't need to know their story to offer this recognition. You just need to remember: they are you, living a different life. They are a soul navigating the human experience, just like you are.

If you practice this throughout your day with everyone you encounter, you won't just feel love. You will be love.

Intention of the Day
I will practice love today with someone outside my inner circle.

All is Well

Ever notice that when you have a negative emotional experience, the muscles in your throat, shoulders, head, belly, or other areas of your body may tighten? Your jaw clenches. Your shoulders creep toward your ears. That's your body preparing for battle—but there's no battle coming. Someone said or did something that upset you, and now your mind is telling your body to prepare for a physical fight that will never happen.

This is your Created Self sounding the alarm. It learned long ago that tension meant readiness, that bracing meant safety. But your Authentic Self knows the truth: most of what you worry about never arrives. And even when challenges do come, you've already proven you can face them. You've survived every difficult day so far. That's not luck—that's evidence.

I experience this pattern in my trapezius muscles—the muscles that run from your neck across your shoulders and down your upper back. Whenever I start worrying about something going wrong, those muscles begin to spasm. It's my body's signal that my mind has wandered into fear. When I notice it, I pause and remind myself: I am already adequately prepared to face whatever comes my way. All is well. Worrying is unnecessary.

Then I do one round of box breathing to release the tension. Inhale slowly for four counts. Hold for four counts. Exhale slowly for four counts. Hold for four counts. That's it. One round. My body softens, my mind quiets, and I continue with my day.

This simple practice—noticing, reassuring, breathing—brings together everything you've explored in this book. Your body communicates; you've learned to listen. Your mind reacts; you've learned to redirect. Your Authentic Self speaks; you've learned to trust it. When you tell your body "all is well," you're not lying to yourself. You're reminding yourself of what's true.

You began this journey asking hard questions about who you really are beneath all the expectations. Now, as you near the end of these pages, remember: you're not the same person who started reading. You've done the work. You've built your toolkit. And whatever comes next, you're ready—not because life will be easy, but because you know how to return to yourself when it isn't.

All is well. And you are well.

Intention of the Day
I will remind my body that we are safe so that peace can replace unnecessary worry.

Your Self-Care Toolkit

Sometimes, when we are very sick, fatigued, or grieving, it can be easy to forget about the many self-care tools we have. A stressed mind is prone to forgetfulness and reduced problem-solving. The very moment you need your tools most is when they slip out of reach.

That's why taking inventory matters. When you write down your self-care practices—and plan how you'll use them—you create a reference you can turn to when your mind is too overwhelmed to think clearly. You don't have to remember everything. You just have to know where to look.

The following pages provide a system for building and using your self-care toolkit.

SELF-CARE TOOLKIT INVENTORY

Start by listing all the self-care tools you currently have. Organize them by how often you use them: daily, weekly, biweekly, or monthly. The "As needed" section captures tools you reach for in specific situations—when stress spikes, pain flares, or emotions overwhelm. For each as-needed tool, note its purpose so you remember when to use it.

I've included my own sample inventory to show you how this works. You'll see my daily practices like Reiki, meditation, and prayer. Weekly tools include gym visits, yoga, and hot baths. Monthly, I schedule massage and chiropractic visits. My as-needed tools—essential oils, tea, tuning forks, my eye massager—each serve specific purposes I've noted beside them.

Use the blank inventory on the following page to create your own. When you see all your tools written out, you may realize you're more equipped for hard moments than you thought.

PLANNING WORKSHEETS

Once you've identified your tools, the planning worksheets help you think through how you'll actually use each one. There's a worksheet for each frequency: Daily, Weekly, Biweekly, Monthly, and As needed.

Each worksheet asks the same questions: Why do you want to use this tool? How will you use it? When will you use it? What do you need to help you use it? What might get in the way? How will you make sure you follow through?

These questions come from health coaching. They help you move from intention to action by anticipating obstacles and creating accountability. Fill out a worksheet for any tool you want to use more consistently.

SUPPLIES CHECK

If a self-care method requires supplies—teas, essential oils, batteries, medications—check that you have enough on hand. Being prepared for unforeseen stressors means having what you need before you need it.

MAKING IT YOURS

The pages that follow include multiple copies of each worksheet to help you get started. Once you've filled these, you can recreate them in a notebook or journal that works for you. Some readers post their completed inventory somewhere visible—on the refrigerator, near their desk, or inside a cabinet door—as a daily reminder of the resources available to them.

Your Authentic Self already knows what helps you feel grounded, restored, and whole. The pages that follow help you gather everything you've learned into a toolkit you can return to whenever you need it.

SELF-CARE TOOLKIT INVENTORY (SAMPLE)

Daily	Weekly	Biweekly	Monthly
Reiki	Gym	Clean car	Massage
Crystals	Pilates		Chiropractor
Meditation	Yoga		Acupressure
Water	Hot bath		
Planner	Foam rolling		
Prayer	Clean home		

As needed	
Tool	Purpose
Essential oils	upper respiratory tract issues, lymphatic drainage
Tea	stress, GI issues, upper respiratory tract issues
Foot massager	foot pain, difficulty falling asleep
Eye massager	eye twitching, difficulty falling asleep
Therapist	Healing trauma
Health coach	Troubleshoot obstacles to self-care

SELF-CARE TOOLKIT INVENTORY

Daily	Weekly	Biweekly	Monthly

As needed	
Tool	Purpose

DAILY SELF-CARE TOOL (SAMPLE): MEDITATION

Why do you want to use it? Simple, relaxes me, and practice improves calming my mind.
How will you use it? Sit in silence for 10 minutes in my living room on the couch.
What time(s) of the day will you use it? 8:45 am
What will you need to help you use it? Solfeggio music and a blanket
What can get in the way of using it? Not having enough time between waking up and starting work at 9:00 am.
How will you make sure you will use it? Wake up at 7:45 am each day, set a reminder alarm at 8:40 am, and place a blanket on the couch the night before.

DAILY SELF-CARE TOOL: ______________________________

Why do you want to use it?

How will you use it?

What time(s) of the day will you use it?

What will you need to help you use it?

What can get in the way of using it?

How will you make sure you will use it?

DAILY SELF-CARE TOOL: _______________________

Why do you want to use it?

How will you use it?

What time(s) of the day will you use it?

What will you need to help you use it?

What can get in the way of using it?

How will you make sure you will use it?

DAILY SELF-CARE TOOL: ___________________________

Why do you want to use it?

How will you use it?

What time(s) of the day will you use it?

What will you need to help you use it?

What can get in the way of using it?

How will you make sure you will use it?

WEEKLY SELF-CARE TOOL: __________________________

Why do you want to use it?

How will you use it?

What day(s) of the week will you use it?

What will you need to help you use it?

What can get in the way of using it?

How will you make sure you will use it?

WEEKLY SELF-CARE TOOL: _______________________

Why do you want to use it?

How will you use it?

What day(s) of the week will you use it?

What will you need to help you use it?

What can get in the way of using it?

How will you make sure you will use it?

WEEKLY SELF-CARE TOOL: ______________________________

Why do you want to use it?
225

How will you use it?

What day(s) of the week will you use it?

What will you need to help you use it?

What can get in the way of using it?

How will you make sure you will use it?

BIWEEKLY SELF-CARE TOOL: _______________________

Why do you want to use it?
How will you use it?
What day(s) of the month will you use it?
What will you need to help you use it?
What can get in the way of using it?
How will you make sure you will use it?

BIWEEKLY SELF-CARE TOOL: _______________________

Why do you want to use it?
How will you use it?
What day(s) of the month will you use it?
What will you need to help you use it?
What can get in the way of using it?
How will you make sure you will use it?

MONTHLY SELF-CARE TOOL: _______________________

Why do you want to use it?
How will you use it?
Which day of the month will you use it?
What will you need to help you use it?
What can get in the way of using it?
How will you make sure you will use it?

MONTHLY SELF-CARE TOOL: ___________________________

Why do you want to use it?
How will you use it?
Which day of the month will you use it?
What will you need to help you use it?
What can get in the way of using it?
How will you make sure you will use it?

Epilogue

I sometimes think back to my time in graduate school—the noise in my head, the pain in my stomach, and the feeling that I was trapped in a life that didn't fit.

If I could go back and whisper to that version of Kelly, I would tell her: It's going to be okay. You're going to find your way out.

But I also want to be honest with you, the reader holding this book. I haven't reached a finish line where everything is perfect. There is no magical destination where the work stops.

In fact, the "Kelly" in these pages represents about seventy percent of who I am—the part of me that is grounded, authentic, and connected to my intuition. But there is another thirty percent of me that still feels ungrounded, uncentered, and uncertain of my own capabilities. There is a part of me that is still learning how to accept the messy, imperfect pieces of myself.

Some days, I am the confident captain of my ship. I stand at the helm with clear skies ahead, trusting my navigation. Other days, the Created Self tries to grab the wheel—and sometimes it succeeds. It steers me toward old patterns: people-pleasing, self-doubt, comparing my progress to someone else's highlight reel. When that happens, I have to gently but firmly take the wheel back. I don't always do it gracefully. But I keep doing it.

I used to think the goal was to be "fixed." I thought that once I healed enough, I would be perfect. That was just another trap.

I am a work in progress. And I realized that the most important word in that sentence isn't "work." It's progress.

As long as I am in progress, I am alive. As long as I am moving—even if it's a spiral that loops back on itself sometimes—I am growing.

You've explored your vehicle, your beliefs, your truth, your trauma, your tribe, your purpose, and your life. That's not small work.

So please don't use this book to strive for perfection. Strive for progress. Strive for the messy, beautiful, ongoing process of becoming who you really are.

You are not broken. You are incompletely built.

And that is exactly where you are supposed to be.

Take a deep breath. Drop the heavy suitcase—**the one packed with beliefs that were never yours**. And welcome to the rest of your journey.

Glossary

Aura. A field of luminous energy that surrounds a person or object. It is often described as a halo of light that reflects emotional or physical states.

Authentic Self. This is the version of a person's identity that represents their true feelings and nature, rather than what society expects them to be.

Biophysicist. A scientist who uses the laws and tools of physics to study how living things work.

Boundaries. Limits you set to protect your time, energy, and well-being. Boundaries communicate what you will and won't accept in relationships and situations. Setting boundaries is an act of self-love that honors your needs as valid and worth protecting.

Calisthenics. Exercises done using only your own body weight, such as push-ups or jumping jacks, to build strength and flexibility.

Cell and Developmental Biology. A branch of biology focused on the structure and function of cells and how organisms grow and develop.

Chakra. A focused center of energy within the body. There are usually considered to be seven main chakras that run along the spine.

Chronic. An illness or problem that persists for a long time or constantly recurs.

Clinical research. A branch of healthcare science that determines the safety and effectiveness of medications, devices, and treatment regimens intended for human use.

Created Self. This is the version of a person's identity that is formed by outside influences, such as family, culture, or society.

Delay-Distract-Decide (3 Ds). A technique for breaking the overindulgence cycle: (1) Delay acting on the urge for at least thirty minutes, (2) Distract yourself with a task that has a clear beginning and end, (3) Decide whether you still need to overindulge after completing the task. The accomplishment triggers dopamine, often reducing the original urge.

Digital Wellness. The practice of using technology mindfully to support rather than drain your well-being. This includes setting boundaries around screen time, notifications, social media, and news consumption to protect your mental and emotional health.

Dopamine. A chemical in the brain that sends signals between nerve cells and is associated with feelings of reward and pleasure.

Energy body. A system of pure energy that mirrors the physical form. It interacts with the environment to support health and filters out harmful forces.

Functional Exercise. Movements designed to train your muscles to work together and prepare them for daily tasks.

Gastritis. A medical condition involving inflammation of the lining of the stomach.

Genetics. The scientific study of genes and heredity, which explains how traits are passed from parents to offspring.

Heart Energy. The emotional quality you bring to any expression of love or care. Heart energy is not a sixth love language but the foundation beneath all five that determines whether actions nourish a relationship or slowly harm it. The same action performed with genuine warmth lands differently than one offered from obligation or resentment.

Irritable Bowel Syndrome (IBS). A disorder affecting the large intestine that causes pain, bloating, and changes in the consistency of bowel movements.

Meridian. A pathway or channel in the body through which energy flows. These paths are similar to how veins carry blood throughout the physical body.

Mindful Eating. The practice of bringing presence and awareness to eating. This includes pausing before meals, noticing hunger and fullness cues, eating slowly, minimizing distractions, and releasing judgment about food choices. Mindful eating reconnects you with your body's wisdom around nourishment.

Pilates. A system of exercises designed to improve physical strength, flexibility, and posture, and enhance mental awareness.

Sedentary. This adjective describes a lifestyle that involves a lot of sitting and very little physical activity.

Semiconducting quantum interference device (SQUID). A very sensitive tool used by scientists to detect and measure extremely weak magnetic fields.

Sleep Hygiene. The habits and environment that support restful sleep. This includes consistent sleep and wake times, a wind-down routine of at least one hour, limiting screens before bed, adjusting bedroom temperature, and avoiding food and fluids close to bedtime.

3-Step Reality Check. A process for examining beliefs that may no longer serve you: (1) Notice the belief and observe it with curiosity rather than judgment, (2) Ask "Is it true?" by examining the evidence for and against it, (3) Ask "Does it help?" by considering whether holding the belief supports your Authentic Self. If a belief isn't true or helpful, you have permission to release it.

Trauma. A deeply distressing or disturbing experience that can have long-lasting emotional effects.

Trauma Response. A behavior or pattern that developed as a survival strategy in response to past wounds. Common trauma responses include people-pleasing, hypervigilance, avoidance, perfectionism, controlling behavior, judgmental attitudes, and victim mentality. These responses made sense when they were needed but may no longer serve your Authentic Self.

Values. A person's principles or standards of behavior that describe what is important in life.

Acknowledgements

This book was shaped by many people and by two countries that are both home to me.

I was born in the United States and raised in Jamaica, and I claim both equally. Jamaica taught me discipline, rhythm, intuition, and respect for the wisdom of the body. The United States taught me endless possibilities and the language of science and healthcare systems. Together, these experiences shaped how I understand healing.

I offer my deepest thanks to my clients and students. Thank you for trusting me with your stories and your healing journeys. Your courage and honesty guided this work more than any method or technique ever could.

I am grateful to my teachers and mentors in energy healing, holistic wellness, and integrative care. Your guidance, care, and commitment to ethical practice laid the foundation for everything shared in these pages.

Thank you to my colleagues and peers for your encouragement, thoughtful feedback, and meaningful conversations along the way. I am especially grateful to those who offered their time, wisdom, and support during the writing and editing process.

To my friends and chosen family in both Jamaica and the United States, thank you for your patience and understanding during the long seasons this book required. Thank you for reminding me to rest and for celebrating each step forward.

I also acknowledge the cultural and ancestral wisdom that informs this work. This book is part of a longer tradition of care that values the whole person—body, mind, and spirit.

Finally, I honor myself for staying with this work. Writing this book required trust, patience, and self-compassion.

May this book offer grounding, reflection, and care to all who read it, wherever they call home.

Notes

INTRODUCTION

Graduate school symptoms and chronic stress

The physiological symptoms of chronic stress in confined or hostile environments—including tension headaches, gastrointestinal distress, muscle spasms, and hair loss—parallel documented effects of prolonged incarceration and toxic workplace environments. Research on psychoneuroimmunology demonstrates how persistent psychological stress manifests in physical illness. See Gabor Maté, *When the Body Says No: The Cost of Hidden Stress* (Toronto: Vintage Canada, 2004), particularly Chapter 3, "Stress and Emotional Competence."

World population

World population surpassed eight billion in November 2022. "Day of 8 Billion," United Nations, accessed January 21, 2026, https://www.un.org/en/dayof8billion.

WHAT IS THE AUTHENTIC SELF?

The concept of the Created Self is discussed in William Lee Rand, *Reiki: The Healing Touch* (Southfield, MI: International Center for Reiki Training, 1991). My understanding of the Created Self builds on this foundation while incorporating insights from trauma psychology and my work as a health and wellness coach. The Created Self, as I define it, encompasses not only cultural conditioning but also adaptive responses to familial expectations, institutional pressures, and individual experiences of fear or trauma.

The Authentic Self as distinct from socially constructed identity draws from multiple psychological traditions. Carl Rogers's concept of the "organismic self" and Donald W. Winnicott's "True Self" versus "False Self" framework inform this understanding. See Donald W. Winnicott, "Ego Distortion in Terms of True and False Self," in *The Maturational*

Processes and the Facilitating Environment (New York: International Universities Press, 1965), 140–152.

For further reading on authenticity and psychological well-being, see Alex M. Wood et al., "The Authentic Personality: A Theoretical and Empirical Conceptualization and the Development of the Authenticity Scale," *Journal of Counseling Psychology* 55, no. 3 (2008): 385–99.

WHAT IS AUTHENTIC SELF-CARE?

The seven dimensions of health

The seven dimensions of health framework—career, physical, mental, emotional, environmental, social, and spiritual—was taught during my training as a National Board-Certified Health and Wellness Coach at Duke Integrative Medicine. This holistic model reflects integrative medicine's approach to whole-person wellness.

Spiritual health as inner peace

The concept of spiritual health as maintaining inner peace and clarity amid life's challenges draws from the Japanese principle of *anshin ritsumei* (安心立命) in Usui Reiki—a state where one's heart is at peace and life's purpose is clear. This principle emphasizes equanimity and centeredness regardless of external circumstances.

SECTION 1: YOUR VEHICLE

Self-Care Tip: Hydrate

Mayo Clinic Staff, "Water: How Much Should You Drink Every Day?," Mayo Clinic, October 12, 2022, https://www.mayoclinic.org/healthy-lifestyle/nutrition-and-healthy-eating/in-depth/water/art-20044256; "Urine Color," Mayo Clinic, accessed January 21, 2026, https://www.mayoclinic.org/diseases-conditions/urine-color/symptoms-causes/syc-20367333.

Stretch for a Happy Body

Mayo Clinic Staff, "Stretching: Focus on Flexibility," Mayo Clinic, February 12, 2022, https://www.mayoclinic.org/healthy-lifestyle/fitness/in-depth/stretching/art-20047931.

Self-Care Tip: Movement Beyond Stretching

For evidence-based guidance on physical activity and its benefits across multiple health dimensions, see the U.S. Department of Health and Human Services, Physical Activity Guidelines for Americans, 2nd ed. (Washington, DC: U.S. Department of Health and Human Services, 2018), https://odphp.health.gov/our-work/nutrition-physical-activity/physical-activity-guidelines. For an accessible overview of functional training principles, see resources from the American Council on Exercise at acefitness.org.

Your Relationship with Food

For readers experiencing persistent struggles with food, eating, or body image that extend beyond Created Self patterns, please see "Self-Care Tip: When to Seek Professional Help" in Section 4. Eating disorders are serious medical conditions that require specialized professional treatment.

Self-Care Tip: Aromatherapy

Imaël Henri Nestor Bassolé and H. Rodolfo Juliani, "Essential Oils in Combination and Their Antimicrobial Properties," in *Molecules* 17, no. 4 (2012): 3989–4006, https://doi.org/10.3390/molecules17043989. This review article summarizes research on the antimicrobial activity of essential oils and their components, including antibacterial, antifungal, and antiviral effects observed in in vitro studies. The authors note that higher concentrations of essential oils may be needed to achieve similar effects in real-world systems compared to laboratory testing.

"Vicks VapoRub—Camphor, Eucalyptus Oil, and Menthol Ointment," DailyMed, National Library of Medicine, revised December 2024, https://dailymed.nlm.nih.gov/dailymed/index.cfm; "Listerine Cool Mint Antiseptic Mouthwash," Listerine, accessed January 21, 2026, https://www.listerine.com/mouthwash/antiseptic/listerine-cool-mint-mouthwash. For comprehensive information on essential oil safety and applications, consult resources from the National Association for Holistic Aromatherapy (NAHA) at https://naha.org .

Self-Care Tip: Weighted Blankets

Baumgartner, Jennifer N. et al., "Widespread Pressure Delivered by a Weighted Blanket Reduces Chronic Pain: A Randomized Controlled Trial," *The Journal of Pain*, Volume 23, Issue 1, 156 – 174.

Keith Zivalich, "Making Something From Nothing: Keith Zivalich of Magic Weighted Blanket," interview by Fotis Georgiadis, Authority Magazine, January 9, 2022, https://www.medium.com/authority-magazine/making-something-from-nothing-keith-zivalich-of-magic-weighted-blanket-on-how-to-go-from-idea-to-e9fa9c9137c7; "What Weight Weighted Blanket Should I Get?," Sleep Foundation, last modified June 21, 2024, https://www.sleepfoundation.org/best-weighted-blankets/weighted-blanket-weight-chart.

Self-Care Tip: Sleep Hygiene

"Sleep Hygiene," Sleep Foundation, last modified August 8, 2024, https://www.sleepfoundation.org/sleep-hygiene; "Blue Light: What It Is and How It Affects Sleep," Sleep Foundation, last modified November 1, 2024, https://www.sleepfoundation.org/bedroom-environment/blue-light.

Breaking the Overindulgence Cycle

"The 3 Ds: Delay, Distract, Decide," Smart Recovery, accessed January 21, 2026, https://www.smartrecovery.org/smart-articles/the-3-ds-delay-distract-decide. This technique draws from cognitive-behavioral approaches to impulse control and is used in addiction recovery contexts. The dopamine response to task completion is well-documented in behavioral neuroscience literature.

Self-Care Tip: Meditate

Meditation apps and resources: Headspace (https://www.headspace.com), Calm (https://www.calm.com), and MyLife, formerly Stop, Breathe & Think (https://www.verywellmind.com/best-mental-health-apps-4692902). For local meditation resources, search for meditation centers, Buddhist temples, yoga studios, and mindfulness-based stress reduction (MBSR) programs in your area.

Clear the Mental Backlog

The metaphor of meditation as "clearing the warehouse backlog" reflects current neuroscience understanding of how the brain processes information. During wakeful rest and meditation, the brain's default mode network becomes active, consolidating memories and integrating experiences that couldn't be processed in real time. See Marcus E. Raichle, "The Brain's Default Mode Network," *Annual Review of Neuroscience* 38 (2015): 433–47.

Self-Care Tip: Digital Wellness

For research on the relationship between digital device use and psychological well-being, see Jean M. Twenge, "Increases in Depression, Self-Harm, and Suicide Among U.S. Adolescents After 2010 and Links to Technology Use: Possible Mechanisms," *Psychiatric Research and Clinical Practice* 2, no. 1 (2020): 19–25. The 20-20-20 rule for reducing eye strain is recommended by the American Academy of Ophthalmology; see "Computers, Digital Devices and Eye Strain," American Academy of Ophthalmology, accessed January 21, 2026, https://www.aao.org/eye-health/tips-prevention/computer-usage.

Self-Care Tip: Journaling

The Forgiveness meditation referenced is from the MyLife app, formerly Stop, Breathe & Think (https://www.verywellmind.com/best-mental-health-apps-4692902).

Understand Your Energy Body

D. Yovan Snanagan Ponselvan, "Introduction to Superconducting Quantum Interference Device," in Advances in Bioelectromagnetism: Innovations and Applications in Healthcare (Elsevier, 2026), 27–41. Superconducting quantum interference devices (SQUIDs) can detect extremely subtle magnetic fields produced by biological processes, including those associated with the heart and brain. While mainstream medicine uses this technology for magnetoencephalography (MEG), complementary medicine practitioners reference it as evidence of measurable biofields.

Self-Care Tip: Get Your Energy Flowing

The concept of meridians as energy pathways in the body comes from Traditional Chinese Medicine, with documented history spanning over two thousand years. For an accessible introduction to TCM principles, see Ted J. Kaptchuk, The Web That Has No Weaver: Understanding Chinese Medicine (Chicago: Contemporary Books, 2000). For information on finding qualified practitioners: National Certification Commission for Acupuncture and Oriental Medicine (NCCAOM) at https://www.nccaom.org; International Center for Reiki Training at reiki.org; National Qigong Association at https://www.nqa.org.

Self-Care Tip: Volunteer

VolunteerMatch is a searchable database of volunteer opportunities by location and interest, available at volunteermatch.org. Many employers offer Volunteer Paid Time Off (VPTO) programs through Employee Assistance Programs (EAPs). Check with your HR department to learn if this benefit is available to you.

Self-Care Tip: Ground & Center

Grounding and centering techniques are found across contemplative traditions, from Taoist meditation to Christian centering prayer. The specific visualization of light and roots described here draws from energy healing practices, particularly Reiki and other Western energy modalities. For exploration of cross-cultural grounding practices, see Tara Brach, *Radical Acceptance: Embracing Your Life with the Heart of a Buddha* (New York: Bantam Books, 2003).

SECTION 2: YOUR BELIEFS

Understanding Where Your Beliefs Come From

The metaphor of beliefs as a "suitcase packed by others" reflects the psychological concept of introjection—the unconscious adoption of others' beliefs, attitudes, and values without critical examination. This concept appears across multiple therapeutic traditions, from Gestalt therapy to psychoanalysis.

Inherited Beliefs vs. Chosen Beliefs

"Spinster," Online Etymology Dictionary, accessed January 21, 2026, https://www.etymonline.com/word/spinster. For historical context on spinsters as valued family members in textile production, see "When Did Spinsters Spin?," Cambridge Group for the History of Population and Social Structure, University of Cambridge, June 12, 2025, https://www.campop.geog.cam.ac.uk/blog/2025/06/12/spinsters.

Questioning Beliefs That No Longer Serve You

The 3-Step Reality Check draws from cognitive-behavioral therapy techniques for examining automatic thoughts and core beliefs. For further reading on CBT approaches, see Judith S. Beck, *Cognitive Behavior Therapy: Basics and Beyond*, 3rd ed. (New York: Guilford Press, 2020).

The Serenity Prayer referenced is commonly attributed to theologian Reinhold Niebuhr and has been adopted widely in twelve-step recovery programs.

Spirituality and Your Authentic Self

For accessible exploration of common threads across spiritual traditions, see Karen Armstrong, *A History of God: The 4,000-Year Quest of Judaism, Christianity and Islam* (New York: Ballantine Books, 1993) and Huston Smith, *The World's Religions* (San Francisco: HarperOne, 1991).

SECTION 3: YOUR TRUTH

Feelings vs. Emotions: Know the Difference

The distinction between feelings (internal reactions to experiences) and emotions (mental and physical responses to feelings) reflects current understanding in affective neuroscience and emotional intelligence research. For further reading on emotional processing, see Marc Brackett, *Permission to Feel: Unlocking the Power of Emotions to Help Our Kids, Ourselves, and Our Society Thrive* (New York: Celadon Books, 2019).

You Are Fine as You Are

RuPaul's Drag Race, season 1, episode 9, "Reunited," aired March 23, 2009, on Logo TV. This phrase has become iconic in LGBTQ+ culture and self-acceptance movements, emphasizing the necessity of self-love as the foundation for loving others.

Feel Everything Fully

For research on how suppressed emotions manifest as physical illness, see Gabor Maté, *When the Body Says No: The Cost of Hidden Stress* (Toronto: Vintage Canada, 2004), particularly Chapter 2, "The Little Girl Too Good to Be True," which documents case studies of patients whose chronic illnesses correlated with emotional suppression patterns.

SECTION 4: YOUR TRAUMA

Recognizing Trauma Responses

The trauma responses described—people-pleasing, hypervigilance, avoidance, perfectionism, controlling behavior—are well-documented in trauma psychology. For an accessible overview, see Pete Walker, *Complex PTSD: From Surviving to Thriving* (Lafayette, CA: Azure Coyote, 2013), particularly Chapter 2, "The 4Fs: A Trauma Typology in Four Types."

Your Body Remembers

Bessel van der Kolk's groundbreaking research on trauma and the body demonstrates how traumatic experiences are stored somatically when they cannot be fully processed psychologically. See Bessel van der Kolk, *The Body Keeps the Score: Brain, Mind, and Body in the Healing of Trauma* (New York: Viking, 2014). For additional reading on body-based approaches to trauma healing, see Peter A. Levine, *Waking the Tiger: Healing Trauma* (Berkeley: North Atlantic Books, 1997).

Let Go of Anger

The story of the hair salon incident reflects a principle discussed in various anger management and mindfulness traditions: the distinction between justified anger and useful action. For further reading on working with anger skillfully, see Thich Nhat Hanh, *Anger: Wisdom for Cooling the Flames* (New York: Riverhead Books, 2001).

Pick Something to Forgive

DMX (Earl Simmons) frequently discussed trusting people to be who they show themselves to be, particularly in interviews about relationships and betrayal. This wisdom—trusting a snake to bite, a liar to lie— appears throughout his public reflections on authenticity and self-protection.

Self-Care Tip: When to Seek Professional Help

Mental health resources: Psychology Today therapist directory (https://www.psychologytoday.com/us/therapists); National Suicide Prevention Lifeline—call or text 988, available 24/7 for anyone in suicidal crisis or emotional distress; Crisis Text Line—text "HELLO" to 741741, available 24/7; National Alliance on Mental Illness (NAMI) Helpline—1-800-950-NAMI (6264), Monday–Friday, 10 a.m.–10 p.m. ET; SAMHSA National Helpline (Substance Abuse and Mental Health Services Administration)—1-800-662-HELP (4357), available 24/7 for treatment referral and information; EMDR International Association (for finding EMDR practitioners)—emdria.org.

Section 5: Your Tribe

The Missing Ingredient in Love Languages

Gary Chapman, *The 5 Love Languages: The Secret to Love That Lasts* (Chicago: Northfield Publishing, 1992; revised 2015). Chapman identifies five primary ways people express and receive love: Words of Affirmation, Acts of Service, Receiving Gifts, Quality Time, and Physical Touch. The concept of "heart energy" as the intention behind these actions extends this framework by addressing the qualitative dimension—how love is given, not just what form it takes.

Section 6: Your Purpose

Make Your Dreams a Reality

David Pogue, "How *Star Trek* Inspired the Future of Tech," *Scientific American*, September 8, 2016, scientificamerican.com/article/how-star-trek-inspired-the-future-of-tech. Star Trek's communicators, PADDs, and replicators—introduced in the 1960s—foreshadowed smartphones, tablets, and 3D printers. See also "Communicator," Star Trek database, accessed January 21, 2026, https://www.startrek.com/database_article/communicator.

Self-Care Tip: Know Your Priorities

The Eisenhower Matrix, also called the Urgent-Important Matrix, is attributed to President Dwight D. Eisenhower, who reportedly said, "I have two kinds of problems, the urgent and the important. The urgent are not important, and the important are never urgent." Stephen Covey popularized this tool in *The 7 Habits of Highly Effective People* (New York: Free Press, 1989).

Worry Reveals Opportunity

Eckhart Tolle, *A New Earth: Awakening to Your Life's Purpose* (New York: Dutton/Penguin Books, 2005), 61. Tolle's teaching emphasizes the futility of worry as a mental habit that creates suffering without solving problems. This aligns with cognitive-behavioral therapy's approach to identifying and reframing unhelpful thought patterns.

SECTION 7: YOUR LIFE

Self-Care Tip: Use Your Hands

Research on hands-on creative activities shows benefits including reduced cortisol (stress hormone) levels, improved focus and present-moment awareness, and increased sense of accomplishment. For an overview of art therapy research, see the American Art Therapy Association's resources at arttherapy.org.

Live Authentically

Gabor Maté, *When the Body Says No: The Cost of Hidden Stress* (Toronto: Vintage Canada, 2004). Maté documents numerous cases where chronic diseases—including autoimmune disorders, cancer, and cardiovascular disease—developed in patients with long histories of emotional suppression and inadequate emotional boundaries.

All is Well

Box breathing technique: Box breathing, also called square breathing, is a controlled breathing technique used by Navy SEALs and other high-stress professions to manage acute stress and regain focus. The practice involves equal counts for inhalation, hold, exhalation, and hold (typically four counts each), creating a "square" pattern. For more on breathwork and nervous system regulation, see James Nestor, *Breath: The New Science of a Lost Art* (New York: Riverhead Books, 2020).

YOUR SELF-CARE TOOLKIT

Planning worksheets and health coaching methodology

The planning worksheet questions—Why? How? When? What do you need? What might get in the way? How will you ensure follow-through?—draw from health coaching methodologies taught in National Board-Certified Health & Wellness Coach (NBC-HWC) training. These questions help move intentions into actionable plans by addressing motivation, logistics, obstacles, and accountability. For more on health coaching approaches, see the National Board for Health & Wellness Coaching at https://nbhwc.org.

GLOSSARY

The glossary provides working definitions as used in this book. For academic or clinical definitions, readers should consult specialized sources in psychology, medicine, and complementary medicine.

Suggested Resources

Authentic Self / Identity / Personal Growth

A New Earth: Awakening to Your Life's Purpose by Eckhart Tolle. A guide to transcending ego-based consciousness and discovering your true self.

Discover Your Authentic Self by Sherrie Dillard. Explores intuitive and psychic approaches to uncovering your authentic identity.

Ikigai: The Japanese Secret to a Long and Happy Life by Hector Garcia and Francesc Miralles. Introduces the Japanese concept of finding your reason for being and living with purpose.

Positive Intelligence by Shirzad Chamine. Teaches mental fitness techniques to quiet your inner critic and strengthen your authentic voice.

Life Values Inventory. Self-assessment tool to identify your core values and how to apply them to daily life. https://www.lifevaluesinventory.org

Trauma / Healing / Emotional Processing

Forgiveness : 21 Days to Forgive Everyone for Everything by Iyanla Vanzant. A spiritual guide to releasing resentment and finding freedom through forgiveness.

Retrain Your Brain by Seth J. Gillihan. Practical cognitive behavioral techniques for managing anxiety, depression, and negative thought patterns.

Relationships / Communication

The 5 Love Languages by Gary Chapman. Explores five ways people give and receive love, helping you communicate care more effectively.

Mindfulness / Meditation / Presence

Full Catastrophe Living by Jon Kabat-Zinn. The foundational guide to mindfulness-based stress reduction from its creator.

Interbeing by Thich Nhat Hanh. Explores interconnectedness and mindful living through Buddhist teachings.

365 Ways to Relax Mind, Body & Soul by Barbara L. Heller. A year's worth of brief practices for relaxation and presence.

Headspace. Meditation and mindfulness app with guided practices for beginners and experienced meditators. headspace.com

Calm. Meditation, sleep, and relaxation app featuring guided sessions, sleep stories, and music. https://www.calm.com

Meditative Mind. Resource for Solfeggio music, meditations, mantras, and sleep music. https://meditativemind.org

Mindful. Articles and resources on mindfulness practices. mindful.org

YouTube. Free videos for guided meditations, stretching tutorials, and self-care practices.

Physical Health / Body Care

Rituals for Transformation by Dr. Peter Borten and Briana Borten. A guided journal combining Eastern wisdom with practical rituals for well-being.

The Five Minute Journal by Intelligent Change. A structured gratitude journal designed to build positive daily habits.

Energy Healing / Spirituality

Reiki: The Healing Touch by William Lee Rand. A comprehensive guide to Reiki practice, history, and techniques.

The International Center for Reiki Training. Reiki education, certification programs, and practitioner resources. https://www.reiki.org

Essential Oils / Aromatherapy

Aromatherapy for Natural Living by Anne Kennedy. Practical guide to using essential oils for health, home, and beauty.

The Plant Guru. Essential oils and aromatherapy supplies. https://www.theplantguru.com

Aromatics International. High-quality essential oils and aromatherapy education. https://www.aromatics.com

Financial Wellness

The Art of Money by Bari Tessler. A holistic approach to transforming your relationship with money through mindfulness and self-compassion.

Professional Organizations / Programs

Duke Integrative Medicine. Integrative health programs, health coaching certification, and wellness resources. https://www.dukehealth.org/locations/duke-integrative-medicine-center

National Board for Health & Wellness Coaching. Find certified health coaches and learn about coaching credentials. https://nbhwc.org

Connect with the Author

My Wealth in Health. Kelly Nembhard's website for coaching, energy healing, and resources. https://www.mywealthinhealth.com

About the Author

Kelly Ayana Nembhard is an energy healer and Authentic Self coach who was born in Miami, Florida and raised in St. Andrew, Jamaica in the West Indies. She graduated from Wesleyan University with a Bachelor of Arts in Biology and from Duke University with a Master of Arts in Cell Biology.

After over 7 years as a clinical research professional, Kelly decided to focus on supporting others in their self-care by becoming a National Board-Certified Health and Wellness Coach. Believing in the benefits of an integrative health lifestyle, Kelly has been devoted to learning and experiencing non-traditional healthcare modalities so that she can be a reliable resource and support for people looking for self-care methods that matter to them.

Kelly's journey led her to become a Reiki Master Teacher, Advanced Crystal Master®, and certified aromatherapist. She has led workshops and taught classes on energy healing and spiritual development and provides one-on-one healing and coaching sessions. Kelly is currently based in Durham, North Carolina and can be found online at www.mywealthinhealth.com.

9 7 9 8 9 9 9 4 7 8 2 3 3 0